Soaring Through the Universe

Soaring Through the Universe

Astronomy Through Children's Literature

Joanne C. Letwinch

1999
Teacher Ideas Press
A Division of
Libraries Unlimited, Inc.
Englewood, Colorado

This book is dedicated to children everywhere with the hope that all will
wish upon the stars and reach for them, too!

TEACHER IDEAS PRESS
A Division of
Libraries Unlimited, Inc.
P.O. Box 6633
Englewood, CO 80155-6633
1-800-237-6124
www.lu.com/tip

Library of Congress Cataloging-in-Publication Data

Letwinch, Joanne C.
    Soaring through the universe : astronomy through children's
literature / by Joanne C. Letwinch.
    xvi, 191 p. 22x28 cm.
    Includes bibliographical references and index.
    ISBN 1-56308-560-7 (softbound)
    1. Astronomy--Study and teaching. 2. Space flight--Study and
teaching. 3. Children's literature, English. I. Title.
QB61.L46   1999
520--dc21   98-53234
                                                      CIP

Contents

4—STAR BRIGHT, STAR LIGHT (continued)

5—TRAVELING THROUGH SPACE 116

6—RESPONDING TO LITERATURE (*continued*)

Acknowledgments

Throughout my many years of involvement in aerospace education, I have been fortunate to have had the support and encouragement of family, friends, and colleagues. I am extremely grateful to all of those people, and wish to extend my thanks and deep appreciation to the following:

The original crew of the New Jersey Young Astronaut Executive Council for their knowledge, energy, and inspiration—Bob, Jerry, Lis, Elaine, Barbara, Janice, Marleen, Greg, and Irene, my friend and assistant in developing and presenting the first workshop that was a precursor to this book;

Haddonfield colleagues—Charlotte, Judy, Toni, Phyllis, and Dolores;

Tatem School Principal, Alan Fegley; Superintendent, Dr. Barry Ersek; and the Haddonfield Board of Education;

All of my students and Young Astronaut participants at Tatem and Central Schools who have been willing to experiment with new ideas, take risks in learning, and exhibit interest and enthusiasm in aerospace science, all of which provided me with the motivation to continue to learn and discover;

My mother, Janet, who other than teaching me my first word, *plane*, instilled in me a love of learning and the importance of continually doing one's best;

My husband, Richard, who has, without fail, given me the *space* to pursue my interest in aerospace science, whether traveling to seminars, attending meetings, or working on a variety of projects (although writing this book definitely pushed the limits).

Introduction

Soaring Through the Universe: Astronomy Through Children's Literature. What a journey! For as long as I can remember, I have been interested in flying, space travel, and the Greek myths. For the past ten years, as I have rearranged my style of teaching to incorporate whole language and literature-based methods, I had often thought about merging the ancient myths and the stars. It seemed so natural, and here and there I would dabble with it but always informally.

Through the years, I have purchased classroom books dealing with all areas of space science, and during the summer of 1994 I took a space science graduate course sponsored by the University of Alabama. The course required writing a unit outline in an area of space science that integrated at least three other subject areas. Earlier that same summer, I had attended classes on Integrated Thematic Instruction, which covered the application of Howard Gardner's ideas on multiple intelligences. The implementation of multiple intelligence strategies became a focal point, and I sensed that now was finally the time to formalize my ideas using mythology, its literature, and astronomy. Thus, *Soaring Through the Universe* was born.

The central idea of this book is the blending of literature and science. Each chapter contains a rather extensive bibliography, focusing on myths and folktales, and offers suggestions for combining these stories with writing, math, science, art, music, and the multiple intelligences. Chapters 1 through 5 are structured so that each can be used on its own or in combination with the others, and each includes introductory literature and response activities followed by a sequential process that leads students through the acquisition of basic scientific understanding within each topic. Chapter 6 contains general recommendations for responding to literature for which most literary works can be accommodated. Following this introduction, there is a list of the multiple intelligences, a lesson plan suggestion, and a short bibliography (see pages xv–xvi).

The responses to literature and other suggestions throughout this book reflect what I have been able to accomplish in my classroom, as well as my individual style of teaching. Use them as guides and modify them to suit your style, comfort level, grade level, and class design.

It has taken me approximately eleven years to gather all the books, materials, lessons, and so forth, to put this program together, so don't feel overwhelmed or overanxious. Start slowly, try a couple of different ideas and lessons, attend a NASA seminar or other aerospace education workshop, and get your feet wet. Relax and have fun. When you see how much the students enjoy the literature and the accompanying activities, you'll be willing to make further attempts.

The concept of *Soaring Through the Universe* started as a few simple star stories and a couple of response-to-literature activities to go with the tales. As you can see, it has become much more than that. My active interest in the Young Astronaut program and NASA's variety of educational opportunities has enabled me to share in a number of outstanding adventures, acquire knowledge, and collect a comprehensive array of materials. Therefore, this book is offered as an introduction to the wide-ranging topic of space science and attempts to share the basics of that topic with you. My wish is that you will find many ways to apply and adapt these suggestions to your style of teaching and be able to discover and share the wonder and excitement of aerospace science with your students.

Using This Book

Space science and exploration have become part of our everyday world. Rarely do space-based projects command the interest of hundreds of thousands of people who stop everything—work, play, entertainment—to watch a launch, as the Apollo program did in the 1960s and 70s. Yet with space-probe launches, the Mir experiments, the Hubble telescope, and the shuttle system, more has been learned about the universe in which we live in the last decade than in all of previous human civilization.

Young students will be growing up in a world where that knowledge, and participation in civil society, will require a vast amount of understanding. Students will help make future decisions about the value and cost of space projects, and many will be participating in them. We cannot wait for students to enter high school or college to have a basic understanding of the universe and space science; it must be the vocabulary of every educated citizen.

It is all the more important, then, to begin to expose young students to the central concepts, science, and literature of a geography that extends far beyond the surface of the Earth. This book is intended as a resource guide to constructing lessons, units, and year-long projects that make the knowledge immediate and gratifying in a way which integrates science, literature, and classroom activity. Because each teacher, classroom, and school require unique directions in the application of such content, each chapter should be viewed as a tool kit from which to build custom lessons and units. Teachers should scan the book, then review each chapter well before classroom activity begins. This allows you, the teacher, to best use local resources (such as identifying and contacting your local NASA Teacher Resource Center), literature easily available in your media center or classroom, combined with computer and multimedia resources, which vary widely. In some schools, every student has access to the Internet and websites. In others, teachers may need to find Internet access and print specific site information to use in the classroom.

Once you have planned your lessons using the resources and ideas provided here, or added other favorites that fit the content, you may use the extensive number of reproducibles in the book to save time and avoid "reinventing the wheel" with each lesson or unit. If you have rarely used astronomy and space science in the classroom, you are in for a "soaring" experience. Teachers experienced with some aspects of the content will find here an integrated approach to multiple activities, as well as myriad ideas for enhancing what you already do. Even teachers who make extensive use of the content will find many new resources and applications, as the information and knowledge available increases almost daily.

Finally, the message of this book is: Have fun! Astronomy and space science are two areas of learning that still bring the joy of discovery and understanding into the lives of students and adults alike.

Happy Skywatching!

Multiple Intelligences:
Definitions and Activities

Intelligence	Definition	Activities
Verbal/Linguistic	Using words and language well both orally and in writing	Reading, writing, memorizing, telling, brainstorming
Mathematical/Logical	Using numbers efficiently and applying logical thinking patterns	Figuring, categorizing, problem solving, number play
Visual/Spatial	Correctly discerning and applying visual/spatial patterns	Drawing, building, map reading, puzzles
Bodily/Kinesthetic	Physical skills, body movement, tactile abilities	Dancing, sports, acting, crafts
Musical	Awareness of rhythm; define and understand musical form	Singing, listening to music, chanting, humming
Interpersonal	Understanding of others	Cooperative grouping, sharing, communicating
Intrapersonal	Understanding of self	Independent study, keeping a journal

(Armstrong, 1994)

Bibliography

Armstrong, Thomas. *Multiple Intelligences in the Classroom.* Alexandria, VA: Association for Supervision and Curriculum Development, 1994.

Gutloff, Karen, ed. *Multiple Intelligences.* West Haven, CT: NEA Professional Library, 1996.

Kovalik, Susan. *ITI: The Model-Integrated Thematic Instruction.* Village of Oak Creek, AZ: Books for Educators, 1993.

Multiple Intelligences Lesson Plan

Name of Lesson _____

Name of Intelligence	Activity
Verbal/Linguistic	
Mathematical/Logical	
Visual/Spatial	
Bodily/Kinesthetic	
Musical	
Interpersonal	
Intrapersonal	

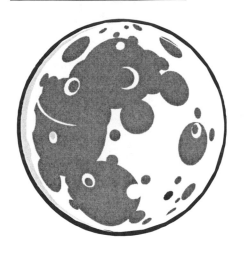

CHAPTER 1

Luna

The Moon

A month prior to starting this unit, have students begin to observe the Moon and its phases. It is better to start during a Full Moon so students aren't telling you, *I don't see anything*. Reproduce the "Moon Phase Chart" (see page 10), distribute it as a homework assignment to be returned on a weekly basis, and enlarge the "Moon Phase Chart" for classroom use. Each week, record the phases and allow students to compare their charts with the classroom chart. Students should make corrections on their own charts if necessary. Be sure to note the name of each Moon phase so that students will begin to familiarize themselves with these names. Emphasize the times of moonrise/moonset, because later you will ask students to *discover* a pattern related to these times and phases. It is important to note that during the waxing gibbous and full moon phases, the Moon will rise in the late afternoon or early evening and set during the early morning hours, which would be the following day. **Example:** Moonrise: 4:00 P.M., Sunday; Moonset: 1:00 A.M., Monday. This may be confusing to students and will require explanation. You may also wish to make adjustments for recording the information on the "Moon Phase Chart." During their observations, students should also look for *pictures* in the Moon. Have them record their ideas on the back of their charts.

Developing Interest

➢   Display a large photograph of the Moon, which you may be able to obtain from your regional NASA Teacher Resource Center (NASA TRC). In addition *Moon, Mars, and Meteorites* has excellent Moon photographs, and *The Young Astronomer* has an excellent map of the Moon on pages 22–23.

➢   Explain that throughout history, people have noticed many different animals/people/shapes in the Moon. Ask students to draw some of the things they may have *seen* during their observations of the Moon, or something they may see *now* as they observe the photographs. Save these drawings for a future writing activity.

The Moon and Fiction

Literature and Moon Pictures

Introduce the book *The Moontellers.* The stories in this book explain pictures seen in the Moon by people of many cultures. Using cooperative pairs or trios, assign one of the stories to each group with the exception of stories one and three. Each group should retell their story by creating a big book page, and each book page should include the following: a map of the region that is the origin of the story, a short retelling of the story, and an illustration. An example follows.

In a Chinese Legend, Rabbit and Frog, Lady Heng-O drank from the Water of Life, and it sent her spinning to the Moon. When the water spilled it turned into a rabbit, and the lady turned into a frog. To this day, the rabbit tries to make a magic potion so that he and the lady may return to Earth. Can you see them?

Each group should present its page to the class, and each page should be saved until the class has completed the next activity. For other stories about pictures in the Moon, refer to "The Hare in the Moon," a tale from India, found in *Tales of the Shimmering Sky*, or an adaptation of "Jakka and Bila," found at the end of this chapter (see page 21).

Writing and Moon Pictures

Now that students are somewhat familiar with Moon legends, it is time to write their own. Using students' prior knowledge, have them name some legend characteristics. Return students' drawings of what they saw when they observed the Moon, and have them plan and write their own legends. When you have all the completed products, gather the original big book pages, add the students' legends, create a cover, and bind them together for your class book explaining what people all over the world observe in Earth's Moon.

The Moon and the Facts

Your students have been observing the Moon and reading tales. It is now time to discover the scientific reasoning behind what they have seen. Use the following cooperative activity adapted from *Advanced Cooperative Learning* to start students thinking about what they know or think they know about the Moon.

➤   Give each student group a sheet of paper entitled, "Our Thoughts and Questions About the Moon."

➤   The students will pass the sheet from person to person in each group, without any discussion.

➤   Each student will write thoughts, and any student may pass if unable to think of something at the moment.

➤   To decide which student begins the process when using cooperative groups, attempt a variety of strategies, such as first name reverse alphabetical order.

➤   An illustration may be used to express a thought or knowledge rather than a written comment, so have a separate piece of drawing paper available for students.

➤   Give about ten minutes to complete this activity, and then have each group select a spokesperson for the group.

➤   As information from each group is explained, post it on a large classroom chart to be displayed and used for reference during the study of the Moon.

Moon Phase Literature

Students should continue to observe the Moon for at least another month or two, while you introduce literature that depicts Moon phases. For lower elementary students, read aloud the Eric Carle story *Papa, Please Get the Moon for Me*, and be sure to allow students to observe the pictures as you read. Have students respond with a response-to-literature activity from Chapter 6, or you may wish to use Carle's book as a listening center activity. Tape the story, have students listen as they read the book, and have them observe the illustrations of the Moon as it changes phases.

Maya Moon is an Aztec legend. This book comes with an audiotape and is probably better for older students. Although it only uses four Moon phases, it delightfully explains how the phases came to be. Other Moon phase stories are "Moon Man," an aborigine story found in *The Moontellers*, and "The Fat Moon," another version of that same story, found in *Legends of the Sun and Moon*. "Weaver Cat" is an Iroquois tale, also found in *The Moontellers*, and "A Gift from the Python" is an African folktale of the Moon phases found in *The Moon in Fact and Fancy*. At the end of this chapter you will find an adaptation of a Norwegian tale, "Jakka and Bila," that attempts to explain the Moon phases, as well as describe pictures in the Moon (see page 21). When using these or any other stories suggested in the book, refer to Chapter 6 to assist you in giving students practice in reading/language skills.

Moon Phase Science

At this point, students should be familiar with the names of the Moon phases and should be making inquiries about how and why these phases occur. Ask students to brainstorm some thoughts and questions regarding the Moon phases and record them. This will also make you aware of students' scientific notions that may be incorrect. Now that students have had a chance to discover for themselves some aspects of Moon phases, use some of the following strategies to allow students to continue developing an understanding of the Moon phase concepts and make corrections to any improper assumptions. Any of these can be done individually, in small groups, or as whole-class activities.

➤ Demonstrating Moon Phases

Introduce students to *The Moon Seems to Change*, and read only to page 19. Based on what they have observed and read, suggest that students create their own demonstration of Moon phases. Make available some materials that students may wish to use, such as flashlights, lamps, oranges, Styrofoam balls, tennis balls, etc. You may also wish to have students plan their activity and have them bring in materials from home for a presentation the following day. Be sure to have students list materials needed and the procedures they will follow.

Recommendations for Moon phase demonstrations can be found in *The Moon Seems to Change* and in *Astro Adventures*. Both work well in allowing students to develop concrete experiences with Moon phases, and the activity in *Astro Adventures* works especially well for older students. When the class has completed a demonstration of the Moon phases, use any of the follow-up activities to confirm students' understanding of how Moon phases occur.

➤ Moon Phase Follow-Up Activities

1. Reproducible: "Matching Moon Phases" (see pages 11–12).
2. Paper Plate Moon Phases. This activity was adapted from one in *Exploration Station*, courtesy of the Teacher Resource Center, Kennedy Space Center, NASA.
    a. Materials needed are small, white paper plates (eight per group, two per student); one yellow and one black crayon or marker per student; eight 3-by-5-inch index cards.
    b. With four students per group, each should complete two paper plates representing two of the Moon phases.
    c. Have each student outline the circle in the middle of the plate with black marker, and based on the Moon phase, shade the circle accordingly.
    d. The yellow crayon should represent the illuminated area of the Moon during each phase, and the black crayon, the area of the Moon that is not illuminated.
    e. The name of the Moon phase should be written on the index card and stapled to the bottom of the paper plate. The phases may be displayed using some of the following suggestions.

➤ *Displaying Paper Plate Moon Phases*

Moon Phase Mobile

Materials needed are a large paper plate, a hole puncher, and some string or colorful yarn. Proceed by punching a hole at the top of each paper plate, attaching a small piece of yarn, and punching eight holes around the edge of the large paper plate.

Thread the yarn from each individual plate through each hole on the large plate and tie.

To create a hanger for the mobile, cut a long piece of yarn, and slip one end through one of the holes at the middle of the large plate, and then through the middle hole on the opposite side. Tie the ends and display the mobile.

Moon Phase Chart

You will need a piece of posterboard that is 18 by 24 inches. Hold it vertically and draw the Sun along the right edge of the posterboard. Draw and label the Earth in the middle. Glue the paper plates in proper phase order around the Earth.

Moon Phase Booklet/Listening Center

Adhere each paper plate to a piece of 9-by-12-inch construction paper. Design a cover and put all the pages together in booklet form. Have students write and record a narrative that names and explains each Moon phase, and place the book and tape in your classroom listening center.

Moon Phase Flip Book

The pattern for this can be found in *Ranger Rick's Naturescope: Astronomy Adventures*, Volume 2, Number 2. To complete this flip book you will need sixteen 3-by-5-inch index cards, a hole puncher, scissors, a brad, and glue. Cut out each of the sixteen sections, and hold each index card vertically. Place the bottom of one section along the center bottom edge of an index card, and glue in place. Repeat for the other fifteen sections. Put the cards in order, punch a hole at the center top of each card, and put the brad through. Students will have a flip book that shows the Moon rotating around the Earth and changing phases.

➤ *Maintaining Understanding of the Moon Phases*

Throughout the year, have students continue to keep daily track of the Moon phases. Most local newspapers carry this information; however, a more precise accounting of the Moon phase on a daily basis can be found at the website *Data Online* available at http://aa.usno.navy.mil/AA/data as of August 13, 1997. Click into *Sun and Moon Data for One Day* available at http://aa.unsno.navy.mil/AA/data/docs/RS_OneDay.html as of August 13, 1997. Record the Moon phase, its corresponding picture, and the rise and set times on a large chart. Perhaps add a saying for the day, a line or two from a poem about the Moon, or an important news or classroom event. If your class is also keeping track of sunrise/sunset times (Chapter 2), after two to three months, have students use their moon-rise/moonset times and sunrise/sunset times to attempt discovery of the pattern that corresponds with these times and the Moon phases. The pattern is:

New Moon: rises and sets at about the same time the Sun rises and sets;

First Quarter: rises about six hours after sunrise and sets about six hours after sunset;

Full Moon: rises near sunset, and sets near sunrise;

Last Quarter: rises about six hours before sunrise, and sets about six hours before sunset.

(Bondurant, 1991)

Moon Phase Poetry

For upper elementary students, consider using four poems by Sara Teasdale. They are entitled, "Moon's Ending," "Full Moon," "Clear Evening," and "Midsummer Night." Each poem depicts a different Moon phase. Have students interpret each poem by painting their visualization of the poem, and label the painting with its corresponding phase. Do the same thing for students in the early elementary grades using the various poems from the book *A Moon in Your Lunch Box*. Look for the these poems: "Full Moon," "How the Moon Gets Smaller," "The Setting Moon," "The Phase I'm Going Through," "In the Distance," "A Moon in Your Lunch Box," "You Can't Be a Full Moon All the Time," and "Tonight's the Moon." In the book *The Earth Is Painted Green*, look for the poem "The Harvest Moon" by Ted Hughes.

More Moon Science

➤ Lunar Eclipse Inquiry

First have students investigate some ancient cultures' beliefs concerning lunar eclipses. Some sources of stories for ancient lunar eclipse beliefs are: *When Jaguars Ate the Moon*, *Mythology and the Universe*, and *The Moon in Fact and Fancy*.

Have students look at pictures of a lunar eclipse. The best sources for these would be NASA photographs, *Sky and Telescope* or *Astronomy* magazines, or the websites for these two magazines. Choose, then, to have students develop an understanding of lunar eclipses using any of the following suggestions.

1. This first idea can be risky because students may develop some incorrect ideas that will need to be corrected; however, it gives students a chance to use prior knowledge, observation, and thinking skills, as well as experiment with different ideas based on prior knowledge, just as real scientists do. You will need to monitor students' work and thought processes very closely. Use the "Lunar Eclipse Inquiry" reproducible (see pages 13–14). Provide students with materials similar to those used to investigate Moon phases. Using their knowledge of how Moon phases occur, request that students create a demonstration showing how and

when a lunar eclipse occurs. Once students have a plan for their demonstration, they should check resources and revise their presentation to make sure that their demonstration is presented accurately.

2. If you'd rather not risk having students develop some incorrect ideas about lunar eclipses, have students investigate their questions on the "Inquiry" reproducible (see pages 13–14) prior to creating a demonstration of how and when a lunar eclipse occurs.

3. Complete a teacher demonstration of lunar eclipses, using either the following proposal, or one that you have devised based on your students' questions. Display the concept of a lunar eclipse by applying the Hula-Hoop idea from *Astro Adventures*, and then have students try this on their own using three balls of clay (different colors) and two plastic bangle jelly bracelets (can be found in the party favors section of most department or party stores). The procedure would be the same as the Hula-Hoop idea, but on a smaller scale. Instead of a student standing in the middle of the hula hoop, use a craft stick inserted into the middle of a piece of clay to represent the person. As you are demonstrating, be sure to have students find the answers to the following questions: During what phase does a lunar eclipse occur? What seems to cause a lunar eclipse? Why doesn't a lunar eclipse occur every month?

➤ *Lunar Eclipse Writing*

As a review, you may wish to have students create a modern tale as to why a lunar eclipse occurs. Most of the ancient tales use fierce animals such as wolves and snakes. Students may want to incorporate up-to-date fictional characters such as Darth Vader, Superman, E.T., etc., and instead of just writing a tale, have students use a play format. Obtain a back copy of the November 1993 issue of *Odyssey* magazine entitled "The Magnificent Moon." The entire issue is devoted to the Moon, both fact and fiction, and I especially like the small excerpts throughout the issue that give information pertaining to each month's Moon from the Native American perspective.

Features of the Moon

The craters, the maria, and the highlands are three of the major features of the Moon. For yourself, refer to background information found in "Exploring the Moon," a NASA resource. For students, an excellent resource is *Our Satellite: The Moon*. Previously students were asked to make observations about the Moon and what they saw when they looked at the Moon. They have heard several accounts of what ancient people thought they observed when they looked at the Moon. Inform students that since astronauts have explored the Moon, we now know much more about the dark spots, the craters, and the light areas of the Moon, and how they probably came to be. The book *Moon, Mars, and Meteorites* also has a good map of the Moon, as well as photographs and drawings of lunar material and geology.

Three NASA activities that work well in developing understanding of lunar geology are entitled, "Lunar Surface," "Impact Craters," and "Clay Lava Flows." Contact your local NASA TRC for these activities that can be found within the "Exploring the Moon" packet, #EP 306.

With the "Impact Craters" activity, I have found that flour works very well, along with cocoa powder as the contrasting color. The white flour and the dark cocoa re-create the dark and light areas of the Moon. If you would like to develop a better understanding of Moon geology, you may want to become certified in using the lunar samples that can be obtained from NASA. Check with your regional NASA TRC for information regarding their Lunar Sample Program.

The Apollo Program

➤ Astronauts on the Moon

Develop interest in America's first landing on the Moon by displaying photographs or old newspaper clippings of the event that took place on July 20, 1969. Again your local NASA TRC will be able to provide you with materials, and be sure to request the videotape of an Apollo launch, which should create interest for your students. Just observing the huge difference between a Saturn V rocket used for lunar launches and today's space shuttle will create much discussion. For photos, check NASA lunar websites and the library or a local science store for magazine photographs.

➤ Apollo Inquiry and Research

Begin the investigation of the Apollo program with a scavenger hunt, and have students work in teams of two. Prepare by writing the answers on sentence strips or flashcards and hide the answer cards throughout the classroom. (Tip: Note where you hide each answer, because it is very easy to forget where you placed them.) Give students the "Scavenger Hunt Questions" (see pages 15–16), and allow approximately twenty minutes to find as many of the answers to the questions as they can. To find the answers to questions that they did not locate, provide resources or assign the remaining questions for homework. The following day, review the answers to make sure everyone has completed the activity accurately, and play a game of Jeopardy for reinforcement.

After the initial investigation regarding the Apollo program, students will have many more questions. Have students list what they already know about the Apollo program, as well as questions they may have. Categorize students' questions and assign one or two questions to each student or pair of students. During the time that the class is working on Apollo research, you may want to consider using the book *Moonwalk: The First Trip to the Moon*, for grades 2–4 as a read-aloud, which provides basic information about the Apollo 11 mission. A good book for older students is *Flying to the Moon: An Astronaut's Story*, written by astronaut Michael Collins, the Command Module Pilot on Apollo 11. Also, from the NASA TRC, try to obtain a video or two regarding the Apollo program.

Students will probably note the way the astronauts are *bouncing* as they walk on the Moon. One question students will probably have come up with during their brainstorming will pertain to gravity. When someone does find out the force of gravity on the Moon, have students determine what their weight would be on the Moon. (Gravity on the Moon is one-sixth that of Earth's gravity.) Also refer to Chapter 5 for gravity activities, as well as additional information and activities regarding space history.

As students complete their research, have them prepare to make their own movie of the Apollo program. Give each team one or two copies of the "Filmstrip" reproducible (see page 18). Team members should illustrate facts pertaining to the questions they researched and include captions. Have one or two students produce a title-page scene and a credits page, and tape all of the scenes together in order. (It is best to tape each piece to the other with masking tape from the back.) Carefully roll up the taped pages, and using two thin dowels, tape the top of your filmstrip, using cellophane tape, along the edge of one dowel. Do the same with the last scene of the filmstrip, and you will have a roll-up filmstrip.

Prepare an audiotape to go along with the filmstrip, by having students make a recording of their captions and adding music and sound effects. As a culminating event to your study of the Moon, invite other classes or parents to a first-run viewing of this original filmstrip. Serve refreshments such as green cheese (whipped cream cheese with green food coloring) and craters (crackers with holes), marbled brownies to represent the dark and light areas of the Moon, and Moon juice (either a root beer float, consisting of root beer and vanilla ice cream, or hot chocolate with marshmallows and/or whipped cream).

Lunar Language

To complete your unit of the Moon, have some fun with "Lunar Language" (see pages 19–20). Consider the following approaches in addition to the one given on the reproducible:

1. Write a riddle book, so that the answer to each riddle is a lunar language word. Give students enough 5-by-7-inch index cards without lines for each riddle, and have them write one riddle and a matching illustration on each card. Make an answer card and a cover card, and bind together all the cards.

2. Create a crossword puzzle using the lunar language words and their definitions. Give students graph paper with one-inch squares and have them practice word processing skills by creating the across/down list of clues on the computer.

Hopefully some of the ideas in this chapter have provided a way to interest your students in studying and observing the Moon, as well as integrating Moon science with literature and language arts skills. Encourage students to continue to explore and learn about the world around them and above them, wherever they may be.

Moon Phase Chart

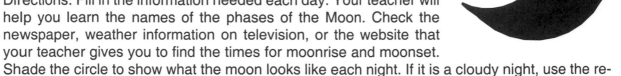

Name _____

Week of _____

Directions: Fill in the information needed each day. Your teacher will help you learn the names of the phases of the Moon. Check the newspaper, weather information on television, or the website that your teacher gives you to find the times for moonrise and moonset.
Shade the circle to show what the moon looks like each night. If it is a cloudy night, use the resources to help you find out what the Moon should look like that evening.

Monday	Tuesday	Wednesday	Thursday	Friday	Saturday	Sunday
Date:	Date:	Date:	Date:	Date:	Date:	Date:
Moonrise	Moonrise	Moonrise	Moonrise	Moonrise	Moonrise	Moonrise
Moonset	Moonset	Moonset	Moonset	Moonset	Moonset	Moonset
Phase	Phase	Phase	Phase	Phase	Phase	Phase

Matching Moon Phases

Name _____ Date _____

Directions:
1. Draw and shade each phase of the moon.

Full Moon

Waning Gibbous

Last Quarter

Waning Crescent

New Moon

Waxing Crescent

First Quarter

Waxing Gibbous

Full Moon

From *Soaring Through the Universe.* © 1999 Joanne C. Letwinch. Teacher Ideas Press. (800) 237-6124.

2. When you have completed step 1, do the following:

   a. Hold a piece of 9-by-12-inch construction paper horizontally.

   b. On the right side, draw the Sun.

   c. In the middle, draw the Earth.

   d. Cut out each Moon phase from this paper, and glue each one in its proper position as it orbits the Earth.

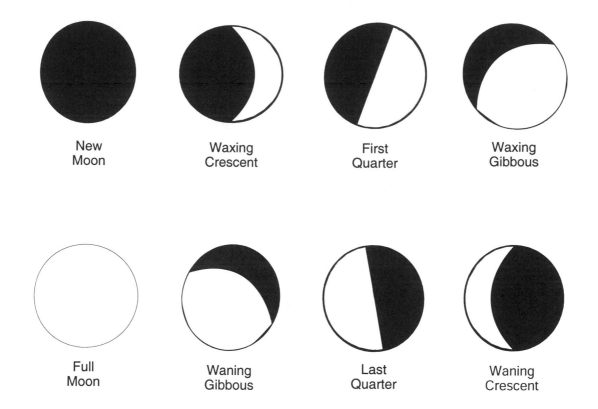

New
Moon

Waxing
Crescent

First
Quarter

Waxing
Gibbous

Full
Moon

Waning
Gibbous

Last
Quarter

Waning
Crescent

Lunar Eclipse Inquiry

Name _____   Date _____

1. Look at photographs of a lunar eclipse.

2. Describe what you see.

    _____

    _____

    _____

3. What differences do you notice, compared with a regular Full Moon?

    _____

    _____

    _____

4. Based on your knowledge of Moon phases, illustrate your thoughts as to how a lunar eclipse occurs.

5. Use resources to check the accuracy of your prediction. How do you need to revise your thoughts as to how a lunar eclipse occurs? Illustrate and explain.

_____

_____

_____

_____

_____

6. List materials needed for an accurate demonstration of a lunar eclipse.

_____

_____

_____

_____

7. Have your teacher check your work before presenting your demonstration of a lunar eclipse.

Scavenger Hunt Questions

Name _____

Date _____

1. What type of rocket was used to launch the Apollo missions?

   _____

   _____

2. There were two sections to the manned portion of the spacecraft used during most of the Apollo missions. What was each one called?

   _____ , _____

3. Up to seven astronauts can fit in the space shuttle. How many astronauts were able to fly on an Apollo spacecraft?

   _____

4. What Apollo mission was the first to orbit the Moon? When did this happen?

   _____ , _____

5. Why was there a setback to the Apollo program in 1967?

   _____

   _____

6. Which Apollo mission was the first to carry and test the lunar module? What were the names of the command module and the lunar module during that mission?

   _____

   _____

7.   What Apollo mission completed the first landing on the Moon? When did this happen?

_____ , _____

8.   What were the names of the astronauts that took part in the first landing on the Moon?

_____ , _____

_____

9.   Who was president of the United States when the first landing on the Moon occurred?

_____

10.   The first American astronaut to go into space also flew on an Apollo mission and walked on the Moon. What was his name? What Apollo mission was it? What did this astronaut do on the Moon that was memorable?

_____ , _____

_____

11.   What was the name of the vehicle that was used during some of the Apollo missions to drive around on the Moon?

_____

12.   How many astronauts have walked on the Moon?

_____

Scavenger Hunt Answers

1. A Saturn V rocket.

2. Command Module (CM) and Lunar Module (LM). The CM held all three astronauts on the three-day trip to the Moon and back. For a lunar landing, one astronaut would stay behind in the CM and continue to orbit the Moon. Two astronauts would detach the LM from the CM and fly to the Moon on the LM.

3. Three.

4. Apollo 8. The actual orbiting of the Moon took place on Christmas Eve, 1968.

5. Three astronauts, Gus Grissom, Ed White, and Roger Chaffee, were killed when there was a flashfire in Apollo 1 during a ground test. This occurred on January 27, 1967.

6. Apollo 9. The command module was called Gumdrop. The lunar module was called Spider.

7. Apollo 11 on June 20, 1969.

8. Neil Armstrong, Buzz Aldrin, and Michael Collins.

9. Richard Nixon.

10. Apollo 14 carried Alan Shepherd. Alan Shepherd was famous for hitting a golf ball on the Moon.

11. The Lunar Rover.

12. Twelve. There have been six successful lunar landings.

(Hartsfield and Norlem, 1983)

Filmstrip Reproducible

Lunar Language

Name _____   Date _____

Part 1: Find the meanings and/or word origins of the following words.

1. lunar _____

2. lunacy _____

3. moonbeam _____

4. honeymoon _____

5. moonlight _____

6. moonstruck _____

7. blue moon _____

8. moonquake _____

9. harvest moon _____

10. moonwort_____

11. month _____

12. Monday _____

13. moonflower _____

14. moonstone _____

15. moonfish _____

Part 2: After completing part 1, use some of the Moon words to write couplets. You may want to use a rhyming dictionary for help.

Examples:

> *When I see a harvest Moon*
> *I walk at night, the moonflower blooms.*
>
>
> *I whistle a happy tune.*
> *The very next day, it's gone at noon.*

Jakka and Bila

An adaptation, written by Joanne Letwinch, of a Norwegian tale.

A long time ago, the Moon was quite different. It was smooth and shiny, like a pearl. There were no dark areas that made pictures in the Moon.

A woodcutter and his wife lived in Norway. They had been married for quite a while before they were blessed with children, twins as a matter of fact, a boy and a girl. The boy's name was Jakka (YAH-kah), which meant *to get bigger*, and the girl's name was Bila (BEEL-lah), which meant *to get smaller*. The family lived on the edge of a deep and dangerous forest, and the woodcutter and his wife tried to protect their children from this dangerous place.

One night, the woodcutter arrived home late from work, and his wife was preparing stew for dinner. She needed some water, but found the water bucket empty. Jakka and his sister volunteered to go to the well for water.

The woodcutter's wife said, "No, you may not go. The well is in the forest, a much too dangerous place at this time of night."

Bila answered, "But Mother, the Moon is bright and full tonight. We are able to see all the way to the well. Look how the Moon lights the way."

The mother observed the Moon as it brightened the path to the forest and allowed the children to go. The children tied a rope to the bucket so they could lower it into the well and off they went along the moonlit path. Their mother watched carefully, and so did the Moon.

"The trees are shining like silver in the Moon's light!" Bila exclaimed.

"The forest is just beautiful with the brightness of the Moon, and it is quite easy to see along this path," Jakka responded.

The Moon heard the children and made himself shine even more brightly.

When they reached the well, Jakka bent over and let the bucket down into the well.

"Oh Bila!" he shouted. "Look, there is another Moon at the bottom of the well!"

What Jakka was really seeing was the Moon's reflection on the water, but he was so amazed that he learned over too far and fell into the well. His foot became entangled in the rope that was attached to the bucket. Running to the side of the well, Bila jumped in to try and rescue her brother. All the while, their mother had been watching. She ran to the well, but she had nothing to use to pull the children out.

The children had been quite complimentary of the Moon, so he felt sorry for them. He was unable to rescue them in order to return them to their mother; however, he was able to send a moonbeam down to the well. The children were able to climb up the moonbeam, but it's path could only lead to the Moon.

So, now you will see Jakka and Bila with their bucket and its rope in the dark areas of the Moon. As you watch the Moon each night, it will grow. At first it will be very small and thin, and as it grows and becomes fatter, you will first see Jakka. As the Moon continues to grow each night, Jakka, Bila, and the rope and bucket will appear, especially when the Moon is full. As the Moon grows smaller again, only Bila is left. She disappears eventually, too, and the Moon becomes a New Moon.

Keep watch over the Moon for a month to see if you can find Jakka and Bila. There are those who think this story also tells the English poem of "Jack and Jill." What do you think?

Annotated Bibliography

Aronson, Bill. *Eclipses: Nature's Blackouts.* New York: Franklin Watts, 1996.
A great resource on lunar and solar eclipses. Excellent photographs.

Asimov, Isaac. *The Moon.* Milwaukee, WI: Gareth Stevens, 1994.
This book gives a wide range of scientific information about the Moon, including how the phases occur and how craters were formed.

———. *Mythology and the Universe* (Isaac Asimov's Library of the Universe). New York: Dell, 1991.

Bondurant, R. Lynn Jr. *Touching Tomorrow: The Moon—Part 1 and 2.* Cleveland, OH: NASA, 1991.

Branley, Franklyn M. *The Moon Seems to Change.* New York: Harper, 1987.
An excellent resource for lower elementary grades. Easy-to-understand explanations and drawings about the phases of the Moon.

Brenner, Barbara. *The Earth Is Painted Green: A Garden of Poems About Our Planet.* New York: Scholastic, 1994.

Bruchac, Joseph, and Gayle Ross. *The Story of the Milky Way: A Cherokee Tale.* New York: Dial Books, 1995.

Brusca, Maria Cristina, and Tona Wilson. *When Jaguars Ate the Moon.* New York: Henry Holt, 1995.
Retold Native American stories about animals and plants in the Americas.

Carle, Eric. *Papa, Please Get the Moon for Me.* Saxonville, MA: Picture Book, 1986.
As a father brings the Moon to his little girl, the phases of the Moon are displayed. This is a delightful first story in which students can observe changes in the Moon's shape.

Collins, Michael. *Flying to the Moon: An Astronaut's Story.* New York: Farrar, Straus & Giroux, 1994.
An updated student version of Michael Collins's tale of his adventures as the command module pilot for Apollo 11.

d'Aulaire, Ingri, and Edgar Parin d'Aulaire. *d'Aulaires' Book of Greek Myths.* New York: Doubleday, 1962.
A variety of Greek myths, including stories of all the major gods, simply retold for elementary-age students.

Donnelly, Judy. *Moonwalk: The First Trip to the Moon.* Random House: New York: 1989.
A very simple storybook that relates the first landing on the Moon.

Estalella, Robert. *Our Satellite: The Moon.* New York: Barron's Educational Series, 1992.
For grades 3–5, good scientific information about the Moon, containing excellent illustrations.

Hadley, Eric, and Tessa Hadley. *Legends of the Sun and Moon.* Cambridge, MA: Cambridge University Press, 1983.
Short, two-page stories that retell legends from various parts of the world about the Sun and the Moon.

Hartsfield, John W., and Shirley M. Norlem. *Lunar Science: Activities for the Elementary Student.* Cleveland, OH: NASA, 1983.

Hillman, Elizabeth. *Min-Yo and the Moon Dragon.* Orlando, FL: Harcourt Brace, 1992.

Krupp, E. C. *The Moon and You.* New York: Macmillan, 1993.
Combining fact with fiction, this book relates short ancient tales of all the natural phenomena, such as phases, eclipses, and tides, related to the Moon. It has charming illustrations along with cartoons that students will enjoy.

Low, Alice. *The Macmillan Book of Greek Gods and Heroes.* New York: Macmillan, 1985.

Retells simply many of the major Greek myths.

"The Magnificent Moon." *Odyssey* (November 1993).
An entire issue dedicated to facts and fiction about the Moon. Includes blurbs about why, according to Native American culture, each month has a particular name for the full Moon.

Milford, Susan. *Tales of the Shimmering Sky*. Charlotte, NC: Williamson, 1996.
Contains various stories about the Moon with suggestions for home and/or school activities.

Mitchell, Marianne. *Maya Moon*. Littleton, CO: Sundance, 1995.
A delightful Aztec tale of how four (First Quarter, Full, Last Quarter, and New) Moon phases came to be.

Moche, Dinah L. *Astronomy Today*. New York: Random House, 1992.

Moroney, Lynn. *The Moontellers*. Flagstaff, AZ: Northland, 1995.
A series of synopses of moon legends from different cultures. Colorful illustrations.

Simon, Seymour. *The Moon*. New York: Four Winds Press, 1984.
Gives simple facts, including the geology of the Moon, how scientists think the Moon was formed, and what astronauts found there.

Slote, Alfred. *The Moon in Fact and Fancy*. New York: World, 1971.

Snowden, Sheila. *The Young Astronomer*. Tulsa, AZ: EDC, 1990.

Spooner, Michael. *A Moon in Your Lunch Box*. New York: Henry Holt, 1993.
A book full of delightful poems, many about the Moon.

Stein, R. Conrad. *The Story of Apollo 11*. Chicago: Childrens Press, 1985.
Starts out with a brief history of the U.S. space program and quickly moves on to tell of the success of Apollo 11. Easy reading for grades 3–5.

Sullivan, George. *The Day We Walked on the Moon: A Photo History of Space Exploration*. New York: Scholastic, 1990.

VanCleave, Janice. *Astronomy for Kids*. New York: John Wiley, 1991.
Many simple experiments dealing with various aspects of the Moon.

References and Resources

Adams, Peter. *Moon, Mars, and Meteorites*. London: British Geological Survey, 1984.

Darling, David J. *The Moon: A Spaceflight Away*. Minneapolis, MN: Dillon Press, 1984.

Exploring the Moon: A Teacher's Guide for Earth and Space Sciences. Washington, DC: NASA, 1994.

Hartsfield, John, and Shirley M. Norlem. *Lunar Science: Activities for the Elementary Student*. Cleveland, OH: NASA, 1983.

Johnson, David W., Roger T. Johnson, and Edythe Johnson Holubec. *Advanced Cooperative Learning*. Edina, MN: Interaction Book Company, 1992.

Schatz, Dennis, and Doug Cooper. *Astro Adventures*. Seattle, WA: Pacific Science Center, 1994.

Young Astronaut Program. *One Small Step*. Vol. 5. Washington, DC: Young Astronaut Council, 1989.

Electronic Sources

Caldwell Lunar Observatory. *Lunar Eclipse Observer Home Page*. URL : http://www-clients.spirit.net.au/~minnah/LEO.html (Accessed July 6, 1997).
Click into images of lunar eclipses, and gather information regarding future lunar eclipses.

Espenak, Fred. *Fred Espenak's Eclipse Home Page.* URL: http://sunearth.gsfc. nasa.gov/eclipse/eclipse.html (Accessed July 22, 1997).

Gives more information on solar eclipses rather than lunar, but has excellent photographs of both types.

Evans, Richard. 1995. *Richard Evans Lunar Home Page.* URL: http://www.trac.net/ users/richare/index.html (Accessed July 6, 1997).

Sophisticated explanations of lunar geology, but click into excellent photos.

Moon Home Page. URL: http://nssdc.gsfc.nasa. gov/planetary/planets/moonpage.html (Accessed July 6, 1997).

Look for lunar images, information on Moon missions, and other lunar science links.

U.S. Naval Observatory. *Data Online.* URL: http://aa.usno.navy.mil/AA/data (Accessed August 13, 1997).

Gives all types of data about the Moon, the Sun, eclipses, and seasons.

U.S. Naval Observatory. *Sun and Moon Data for One Day.* URL: http://aa.usno. navy.mil/AA/data/docs/RS_OneDay. html (Accessed August 13, 1997).

Use this to get specific sunrise/sunset and moonrise/moonset times for your location. Gives Moon phase information as well.

CHAPTER 2

Del Sol

The Sun

Introduction

A beautiful, bright sunshiny day! Who doesn't enjoy such a perfect day? Most everyone does of course, but did you ever stop to wonder about the powerful effect the Sun has on our daily lives? Of course, it is really Earth's daily rotation and yearly revolution of the Sun that affects our daily lives—the weather, the seasons, the number of daylight hours, how one may feel on a particular day or during a particular season, but I would venture a guess that most people view those matters in terms of the Sun. Therefore, it is important to understand the potent force of the Sun and its effect on much of what we do.

Following are some suggestions that may help to generate interest among your students in a study of the Sun.

1. Have students first create their own folders entitled "The Sun" so that all appropriate papers, pictures, etc., can be stored in the folder.

2. Display a large photo of the Sun, using, perhaps, the photos in Seymour Simon's book *The Sun*, or NASA photographs obtained from your regional TRC, and explain to students that you are asking them to observe the Sun using a photograph, because it is unsafe for anyone to look directly at the Sun, even with sunglasses. Excellent photographs can also be found online at the following websites: *The Sun: A Pictorial Introduction* found at http://www.hao.ucar.edu/public/slides/slides.html and *The Virtual Tour of the Sun* found at http://www.astro.uva.nl/michielb/od95.

3. Give students a piece of paper entitled, "My Thoughts About the Sun," and have students brainstorm their reflections, feelings, and experiences with the Sun. When students have completed this activity, record their impressions on a class chart, allowing the chart to be available for students to insert drawings.

4. In lieu of a class chart, note students' brainstorming thoughts on the classroom word processor, save it, and have students insert appropriate clip-art pictures when they have some extra time. If possible, have students each make their own page by inserting clip-art on the saved page, printing it, deleting the artwork, and leaving the printed page for another student to add artwork and print the page.

For students to understand the strength and energy of the Sun, read aloud the Greek myth of Phaethon and Helios. This story can be found in *d'Aulaires' Book of Greek Myths*, *The Macmillan Book of Greek Gods and Heroes*, and as the myth "Chariot of the Sun God" in *Favorite Greek Myths*. As a response to this story, have students create a storyline, directions for which can be found in Chapter 6.

Your study of the Sun will proceed based on some of the questions and/or thoughts your students have; however, this chapter will give you some ideas on how to enhance that study using literature and basic information about the Sun.

Solar Investigations

Fun Facts

Choose from any of the following activities, using the "Solar Jeopardy" and "Sun Questions" reproducibles (see pages 37–38), to interest your students in learning some facts about the Sun.

1. Complete a Jeopardy-type activity using the information on the "Solar Jeopardy" reproducible by making sets of question and answer cards for each group of two or four students in your class. Have students match the questions and answers they think would go together. Display a number of fact books about the Sun so that students may check their answers, and have them match the cards until all of the correctly paired answers and questions are recorded on the "Sun Questions" reproducible. As a follow-up, have each pair or group of students complete a frame booklet about Sun facts.

2. Frame Book

    a. Present groups of students with copies of the "Frame Book" reproducible (see page 39), and divide the facts from the "Sun Questions" reproducible among the groups so that each group has one or two different facts. Each group will then complete one frame book page for each of its assigned facts (see step b below), and all the pages can then be assembled to make one class booklet about Sun facts. If you wish, save this activity for later during the unit, when more investigations have been completed and additional facts about the Sun are known.

      This activity was adapted from *Activities for Any Literature Unit*, which has several different ideas for student publishing.

    b. To accomplish the frame book tasks, have students illustrate a fact about the Sun in the center frame area, perhaps drawing and then painting with watercolors, or perhaps using a crayon wash. Around the outside of the frame, students should write, in a sentence or two, the fact that the picture illustrates. Create a cover for the book and bind the pages together.

3. Use an overhead projector and transparencies as another way of allowing students to investigate some facts about the Sun. Prepare by making enough copies of the "Sun Questions" reproducible for each student, and using the information from the "Solar Jeopardy" reproducible, write each answer on a transparency. Display one answer at a time on the overhead projector, have students select the question to which they think the answer matches, and write the answer in the

space provided underneath that question. Using the investigation suggestion in activity 1 of "Fun Facts," have students determine the accuracy of their answers.

4. Separating the book into three sections, read aloud Seymour Simon's book *The Sun*. Because his books usually do not contain page numbers, the first section ends with the sentence "Still the Sun has enough hydrogen to continue sharing for another five billion years." The second section talks about the parts of the Sun, and the third section concerns activities that take place on the Sun. As you finish reading each section, carry out the following activities.

   a. First section. Complete the activity described in the reproducible "Solar Facts" (see page 40).

   b. Second section. Complete the activity from the reproducible "Parts of the Sun" (see pages 41–42).

   c. Third section. Divide the class into small groups of at least three per group. Each student in the group should assume the role of one of the activities of the Sun—a flare, a prominence, and a sunspot. Each student should create a very simple costume to exhibit its *character* and a placard with two to three sentences indicating what it does on the Sun. Students should need no more than fifteen minutes to prepare, and each group should then present their portrayal of the Sun's activities.

Literature and the Sun

There are several stories about how light and the Sun came to be, or how the Sun came to be in the sky. From *Legends of the Sun and Moon* try these stories: "The Bonfire," an Aboriginal story; "The Fifth and Final Sun," a Mexican story; and "Sun, Moon, and Water," a Nigerian story. The Nigerian story can also be found in picture book form, *Why the Sun & Moon Live in the Sky*. *Er-Lang and the Suns* is a short Chinese folktale relating how the Sun came to be in the sky for only part of the day, and from *Tales of the Shimmering Sky*, read "The Division of Night and Day." After students have listened to or read some of these stories, undertake some of the following activities.

1. The Sun Has Begun. Use this as the headline for a newsletter based on any of the above listed stories. Have students write news articles and editorials about the behavior of some of the characters or the situations that occurred, and include advertisements and a comic section. To assist students in starting their writing, and to practice word processing skills, use any newsletter template found on most word processing programs.

2. Many of the Sun myths and legends involve some type of conflict. After reading one of these, have students list the characters and their traits, state the conflict that took place, and determine the steps taken to solve the problem. Students should express and support their opinions as to whether or not they agree with the solution to the problem, then discuss or write suggestions that resolve the conflict differently, taking into consideration the behaviors and traits of the characters. Students may be interested in setting up a debate to deliberate the pros and cons of the conflict resolution suggestions, or you may suggest that students act out the resolutions and vote on which one works the best.

3. This next activity provides practice with letter writing, while following the conflict theme. Have students work in pairs. One student should assume the role of Dear Abby, and the other should play the role of a character from one of the stories, preferably one who has a major problem. The story character should write a letter to Dear Abby explaining the problem and asking for help. The student playing Dear Abby should answer the character's letter with a sensible resolution to the conflict. That resolution may be different from the one in the story, but should complement the basic storyline of the Sun becoming part of the world.

Sun Science

Students now know the parts of the Sun and some legends of the Sun; therefore it is time to find out what the Sun does and how it behaves. Following are a variety of ideas from which you may choose or combine.

1. Keep track of sunrise and sunset times for an entire school year. Do this on a weekly basis because the times change only slightly each day, and have students calculate the difference in daylight time each week. Check the local newspaper for this information, or tap into the *U.S. Navy Sun and Moon Data for One Day* website located, as of August 13, 1997, at http://aa.usno.navy.mil/AA/data/docs/RS_OneDay.html. Beginning in September, focus on how the daylight time becomes shorter until the Winter Solstice, and from that point, emphasize how the daylight times become a little bit longer each week until the Vernal Equinox. If you are still in school almost until the Summer Solstice, continue to keep track, and give students a chart to take home for the summer so they become aware that daylight time begins to shorten again soon after the Summer Solstice. An example of a "Sunrise/Sunset" recording sheet found at the end of this chapter will assist your students in this activity (see page 43). In a later section in the chapter, you will be able to use this activity to discuss how the four seasons occur.

2. To correspond with the above activity, have students make a sundial. The main purpose of this is to keep track of how the shadow of the Sun changes throughout the seasons, and again, you may want to do this only once a week. Suggestions for making and using sundials can be found in several different sources, such as *Keeping Time*, chapter 2; from The Young Astronaut Program, *Ulysses: A New View of the Sun*; *Exploring the World of Astronomy*, and *Touching Tomorrow: The Sun*. The latter gives an excellent graph on which student can keep track of the daylight hours and easily track its ups and downs throughout the seasons.

    To use the sundials your students have made, attach a piece of paper to the sundial and trace the shadow line each hour. Date each paper and post the weekly sheets for a month. At the end of each month, have students make observations as to the length of the shadows, how they have changed, and how the shadows have changed along with the hour. Be sure to have students connect their shadow observations with sunrise/sunset times and seasons.

3. Another possibility is to have students trace each other's shadow once every three months or so. Follow this timeline: the first day of school, the day of the Autumnal Equinox (or closest sunny day), the day of the Winter Solstice, the day of the Vernal Equinox, and a day when school is still in session that is as close as possible to the Summer Solstice. Be sure to do this each time at the same time of day and face North. Students should cut out their shadows and label each one with their name, date, and time the shadow was traced. As you add to the shadows, staple them on top of one another, discuss the differences, and investigate the reasons why these differences occur, such as time of day and year, the Earth's position, and the position in which we see the Sun. Display the shadows in the classroom.

Solar Eclipses

Introduction

Display some photographs of a solar eclipse. Two excellent photos can be found in Seymour Simon's *The Sun*, as well as in astronomy magazines such as *Astronomy* or *Sky and Telescope*. Contact your local NASA TRC for photos that they have available, or check the websites listed in this chapter under "Solar Eclipse Science" (see page 32). Request that students record their observations and critique with students what they have detected.

Solar Eclipses and Literature

As we have seen with the Moon, ancient people were fascinated by the nature of the Moon, and the same is true of the Sun. Many ancient civilizations worshipped the Sun. The Egyptian Sun god was Ra, who was considered the protector of Egypt. The Babylonian Sun god was Shamash, who gave laws to the people, and the Greek Sun god was Helios, who drove a golden chariot across the sky.

Ancient people did not have the knowledge that we have about the nature of a solar eclipse, so when one did occur, most legends from ancient civilizations depict people becoming frightened. Some civilizations felt that the gods were angry with them; others thought the Sun was being chased by dragons or other monsters, and when the dragons caught up with the Sun, the dragon would try to swallow it. By banging on drums and making as much noise as possible, people hoped that the dragons would be frightened and go away. Of course, it worked, because the Sun would always return. Occasionally, ancient civilization legends referring to a solar eclipse predict that something positive was about to happen, but this was usually not the case.

Before reading any eclipse legend, students may want to think about and record their thoughts about what they may have wondered long ago as a solar eclipse occurred. As a class or homework assignment, have students write two paragraphs by completing their thoughts regarding the following two statements:

If I had lived in ancient times and had viewed a solar eclipse, I may have felt . . .

If I had lived in ancient times and observed a solar eclipse, I might have predicted . . .

In the first paragraph, students should describe feelings they may have had and why. In the second paragraph, a description of what may have been happening in the world of nature during a solar eclipse should be described.

To promote listening skills, have each student choose one of their two paragraphs to read to a partner. The partner who has been the listener should write, in his own words, his partner's thoughts, using the "Sunshape" reproducible (see page 44). Partners should then switch roles. The sunshapes may be colored, decorated, and put together into a classroom book so that all classmates may read one another's ideas.

Read with students *Sunpainters: Eclipse of the Navajo Sun*, and use the reproducible of the same name (see pages 45–46) before, during, and after the reading. Examine the questions on this reproducible beforehand, so that students will be able to think about them as the story is read. Stop at regular intervals to allow students to reply to some questions and discuss some of the circumstances as they occur. Additional story response suggestions are as follows:

> ➢ Have students work in groups of three and pretend that they are visiting the Navajo reservation of Kii and Pipa during a solar eclipse. If you have worked with students on how to write dialogue, review some aspects of this skill, and request that students write a dialogue among themselves, Kii, and Pipa. (See Chapter 6 for dialogue writing suggestions.) Each student in the group should take a role—one student as Pipa, one as Kii, and one as the visiting student—and work together to write the conversation that could possibly take place among the three characters. To have students share their dialogue writing with their classmates, have each student create a mask that represents her character, using the mask to cover only the nose and eyes. Students may then wear their masks as they demonstrate their conversations as Kii, Pipa, and the student. Use posterboard to create the masks and elastic bands to form the headbands.

> ➢ Illustrate, in sequence, what Kii observed during the solar eclipse. Use watercolors, posterpaints, crayons, etc.

> ➢ Produce a poster that lists adjectives or descriptive phrases from the story. Draw a line down the middle of a 12-by-18-inch piece of posterboard to form two columns. List the adjectives or descriptive phrases on one side and illustrate the words and statements in the other column.

Sun and Moon, a delightful story of friendship that results in a solar eclipse, and "The First Eclipse," a Japanese folktale, are two other accounts that can be used to interest your students in studying eclipses. *Sun and Moon* can be enjoyed by students of all levels. The Japanese folktale, which can be found in the book *Myths and Legends* by Anthony Horowitz, is better used by older students. Because of the many gruesome details in this folktale, I have written an adaptation (see page 31) eliminating those aspects, leaving you with the choice of using the original or the adaptation. See the "Movie Time" retelling idea in Chapter 6 (see page 155) as a possible response activity to these stories.

The First Eclipse

a Japanese myth
adapted from *Myths and Legends*
retold by Anthony Horowitz
(edited by Joanne Letwinch)

Susanoo, the Japanese god of the sea, weather, and fertility, and his sister, Amaterasu, the goddess of the sun, came to life in a most unusual way. Their father, Izanagi, the first Japanese god, had just visited his dead wife in the Underworld. Expecting to see her as she was when she was alive, he was shocked to witness a most unpleasant sight. Izanagi's wife was no longer beautiful, but a perfect skeleton with worms for eyes. Izanagi ran away screaming and threw himself into the ocean to rid himself of this horrible sight. The icy cold sea cleansed Izanagi's brain, and he soon forgot the ghastly sights he had viewed.

However, as these visualizations were being washed away from their father's head, from within his thoughts and the bubbles of the sea, Amaterasu and her brother, Susanoo, were born. Susanoo's name means, "swift, headstrong god," and he continually argued with his father until he was thrown out of his father's home and forced to live in the territory of Izumo near the Sea of Japan. Amaterasu, as the sun goddess, had long lived in the sky, so Susanoo decided to pay her a visit before going to live in Izumo.

Susanoo, being thoroughly excitable and emotional, caused quite a commotion when he visited his sister. He began to ruin the Earth, demolishing rice fields and a temple, and injuring his own horse. As he threw his horse into the air, it landed on the roof of Amaterasu's house. Her house, and everything and everyone in it, was destroyed. Amaterasu was so frightened that she ran out of her house and into a dark cave. She hauled a huge boulder across the entrance of the cave so that no one could enter. Because she was the goddess of the sun, the Earth was immediately immersed in darkness. **And so the first eclipse occurred.**

Although Susanoo was punished for his actions by the other gods of Japan, they now had a tremendous problem on their hands. They needed to get Amaterasu out of the cave so that she could bring light to the world once again. All the gods had many ideas, but the god named Treasure-thoughts was the one whose inspiration worked.

The gods decorated a Sukaki tree that was outside the cave with beautiful jewels, ribbons, and mirrors, and they sang and danced as if a religious celebration was taking place. As Amaterasu heard the noise, she peeked out of the cave and was amazed at what she saw. Curiosity got the best of her and she wanted to see more. She slowly moved out of the cave, and as she did, the jewels glowed brightly and the ribbons blazed with color. As Amaterasu moved even farther away from the cave, the god of force used his strength to power the boulder back in front of the cave, tying it down so that Amaterasu could not return. Amaterasu realized at once that she had been fooled into coming out of the cave. She was angry at first with the other gods for this, but she was entranced with the beauty and impressed with how the gods had thought to deceive her. She agreed to return to the sky and light the world. **So ended the first eclipse.**

Solar Eclipse Science

Review what students already know about a lunar eclipse. Based on this information, have students brainstorm the differences between a solar and lunar eclipse, using "Solar Eclipse Brainstorming" and "Solar Eclipse Science" (see pages 47 and 48).

Analyze this assignment with students and remind students of the lunar eclipse demonstration ideas from Chapter 1. An excellent source of information for teachers is the "Educator's Guide to Eclipses" published by NASA's Jet Propulsion Laboratory. Define a solar eclipse with students and allow them to act out or demonstrate their ideas on solar eclipse occurrence. Are their ideas possible or not? Why/why not? Permit students to make changes in their presentations, and be sure that all groups eventually present a correct demonstration of a solar eclipse. Preferred resources for students are: *Eclipse: Darkness in Daytime*; *The Young Astronomer*; and *Eclipses: Nature's Blackouts*, as well as the following websites: *Skyonline Eclipse Page* at http://www.skypub.com/eclipses/eclipses.shtml; *The Eclipse Chaser-Guide to WOW* at http://www.eclipsechaser.com; *Fred Espenak's Eclipse Home Page* at http://sunearth.gsfc.nasa.gov/eclipse/clipse.html.

As follow-up activities, suggest that students choose one, or a combination, of the following ideas, to be completed individually or in small groups.

➢ Create a dramatization employing ancient ideas of the *science* behind a solar eclipse and current knowledge. The dramatization should show a clear understanding of how and when a solar eclipse occurs.

➢ Use the same comparison/contrast idea, except have students produce a comic book.

➢ Write poems and/or songs based on *their experiences* with solar eclipses in both ancient and modern times.

➢ Compose and illustrate two letters to a friend based on solar eclipse experiences, again one in ancient times, and one in modern times.

Solar Eclipse Vocabulary

Using previously mentioned sources, the reproducibles "Solar Eclipse Science" and "Solar Eclipse Vocabulary" (pages 48–49) as well as the *Dictionary of Astronomy*, create a solar eclipse vocabulary list for students. Students may create a Memory- or Concentration-like game using words and pictures to practice this new vocabulary, or they may create their own "Sun-box" in which word, definition, and picture cards are kept. From this box, cards can be drawn by a student while one or two others in a group state a matching word or definition.

Solar Viewing

As previously mentioned, students should be reminded of the dangers of observing the Sun **at all times**, even, and especially during, a solar eclipse. **Never** observe the Sun with the naked eye. See *Tales of the Shimmering Sky* and the NASA teacher's guide *Space-Based Astronomy* for suggestions on how to build a pinhole viewer. The July/August 1991 issue of *Odyssey* magazine has solar eclipse photos, vocabulary, and viewing information.

Sunlight and Science

Lights! Colors! Rainbows!

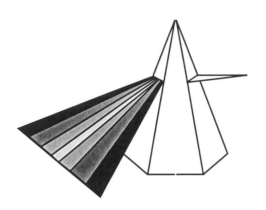

What would a study of the Sun be without some attention given to visible light, color, and rainbows? On a beautiful, sunny day, especially in spring, take students outside to scrutinize and illustrate some of nature's colors. Take a large piece of white mural paper with you, place it on the sidewalk, permit students to line up and kneel down along the paper claiming their own illustration area, and have students divide their area into seven sections. Invite students to look for a natural object that is red and portray it in one of their sections. To further inspire their thinking of **red**, as the students are drawing, read aloud the section on **red** from *Hailstones and Halibut Bones.* When students have completed the **red** object that they have selected to illustrate, ask them to draw other items in nature that come to mind that are **red.** Be careful not to let students know that you are concentrating on the colors of the rainbow; they may discover that themselves at some point. Continue this process for all the colors of the rainbow. Display the finished product in your classroom, or cut it apart so that each student will have his own piece of nature, but be sure to save the artwork for the rainbow writing activity that follows.

Hopefully, the following day is another beautiful, sunny day. If so, take students outside again and have each student bring a box of crayons, a pencil, and a circle of white posterboard, about two inches in diameter.

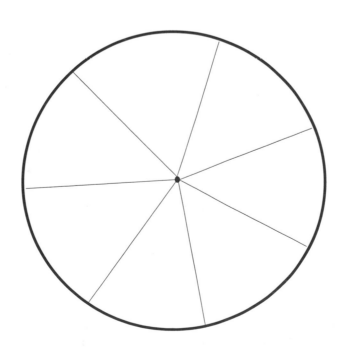

With students working in small groups, give each group a prism, and request that each student divide the white circle into seven sections, pizza style. Students should look through the prism and shade a section of the circle for each color observed through the prism. All the colors of the rainbow should be witnessed (ROY G. BIV: **R**ed, **O**range, **Y**ellow, **G**reen, **B**lue, **I**ndigo, and **V**iolet), however students may miss indigo because that is often difficult to see. Once students have completed the coloring of their circles, have them put a pencil through the middle, spin the circle as quickly as possible, and respond to the questions on the reproducible "Discovering White Light" (see pages 50–52). They should notice that as the circle spins, it appears to turn white. (This activity was adapted from *Ulysses: A New View of the Sun*, a Young Astronaut Council activity.)

For the next activity, set up an overhead projector, which, of course, emits white light. Use a small square of diffraction grating, obtainable from a science supply company, such as Edmund Scientific. Frame the diffraction grating square with a bit of posterboard so that you have what amounts to a small slide, and tape this slide in front of the light on the overhead projector. Have students again respond on the "Discovering White Light" reproducible, noticing that the white light of the projector becomes a rainbow.

After completing all the activities, follow with a discussion of visible light and how it is bent to form the colors of the rainbow. You may want to have students conduct other bending-of-light experiments, for example, with bubbles and rainbows, or make a spectroscope. Further information on all of this, as well as additional projects on light and rainbows, can be found in *Lightning and Other Wonders of the Sky*, *Tales of the Shimmering Sky*, *Astronomy for Every Kid*, and *Space-Based Astronomy: Teacher's Guide with Activities*. The book *Wonders of Science* furnishes easy-to-understand information and simple experiments on eclipses, light bending, and how light produces a blue sky. One rainbow website is *Rainbow Maker Home Page* found at http://www.zianet.com/rainbowhome.htm. Topics such as "How Rainbows are Formed," "How to Make a Rainbow," and "Rainbow Mythology" can be found there. *Rainbows by Randy Wang* is another good website that contains color photos and poems. It can be found at http://http.cs.berkeley.edu/~rywang/magic_small/rainbows.html.

Rainbow Writing

While students are in the process of experimenting with light and rainbows, engage them in a writing and art activity devising their own rainbow simile poems. The following procedure is suggested.

> ➤ For poem topics, make a list, with the class, of items that come in many different colors, preferably the colors found in rainbows. Some examples are: flowers, balloons, Skittles, Popsicles, fireworks, tropical fish, tropical birds, gelatin, jellybeans, etc.

> ➤ The title of each rainbow poem will be *A Rainbow of* _____ , and the student will fill in the blank based on the topic chosen. As an example, I will use *A Rainbow of Balloons*.

> ➤ Next, instruct students in the art of writing similes (Chapter 6). To assist in generating ideas, refer back to the original artwork the students created when they illustrated the colors of the rainbow.

➤   Compose a few lines of a simile poem with the students as an example.

A Rainbow of Balloons
As red as a fresh-picked cherry.
As orange as a blooming tiger-lily.
As yellow as a golden sunset.

➤   Give students a chance to choose their topics and jot down ideas for similes.

➤   Be sure to emphasize the use of a thesaurus.

➤   Once students have completed their similes, they are ready to make their rainbow.

The following will assist in having your students produce their rainbows.

➤   Students will use a 12-by-18-inch posterboard or heavy white construction paper and draw seven concentric arcs to illustrate a rainbow shape.

➤   Within each arc, write a simile for each color, following the order of the rainbow colors.

➤   Have students outline each arc and color within the arc using the colors of the rainbow.

➤   Allow students to be somewhat creative with their coloring and design of the rainbow, but be sure that they comply with the basics of rainbow color and order.

➤   Cut out the rainbow, and from the remaining paper, draw and cut out two clouds.

➤   Attach one cloud to the front end of the rainbow, instructing students to write the title of their simile poem and their name on it.

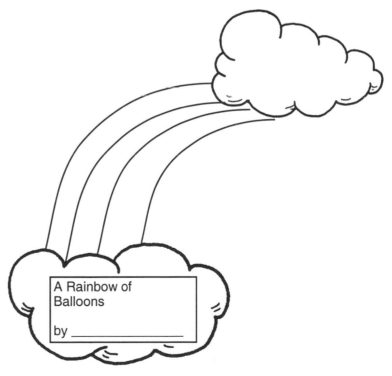

➤   Affix the second cloud to the other end of the rainbow, directing students to decorate the cloud with pictures of the rainbow topic, such as the balloons.

➤   Arrange the completed rainbows around the room for a bright, spring display.

The Seasons

The last topic that you may want to consider during a study of the Sun is the exploration of the way that day, night, and the seasons occur. Earlier in this chapter, it was suggested that students maintain a record of sunrise/sunset times and chart and graph the differences. This will stimulate interest in understanding two very abstract concepts, the rotation and the revolution of the Earth around the Sun. Ask students to recall differences they have noted throughout the year in seasons and in daylight/nighttime hours, and refer to their shadow differences as well.

The fact that the Earth is tilted at an angle of 23.5 degrees, and how that tilt effects the changes in seasons, is an important concept for students to understand. Using your classroom globe is probably one of the better ways to illustrate this point, or undertake the demonstration described in *Tales of the Shimmering Sky*, using the story "The Twelve Months" and the corresponding activities.

Literature and the Four Seasons

Literature with the four seasons as a topic is plentiful. The story of Demeter and Persephone, a Greek myth, tells how the seasons came to be, and can be found in *Favorite Greek Myths*, *The Macmillan Book of Greek Gods and Heroes*, or *d'Aulaires' Book of Greek Myths*. Using the suggestions on paragraph writing in Chapter 6 would work well using the four seasons. Have students write paragraphs describing the four seasons, illustrate the four seasons, and illustrate scenes from any of the seasons stories. A very simple picture book, *The Reasons for the Seasons*, can be shared with students.

The four seasons is also a popular poetry topic. Your school or local library has an abundance of children's poetry books, and I have listed several in the bibliography that I have found to be particularly helpful. Select a poem or poems about each season, or have students research and find a variety of poems that they enjoy about each of the seasons. Assign this task individually, as a long-term project, or complete in class using cooperative groups. Following is a suggested student response to the poetry.

➤ *Poem Palettes*

Poetry is a work of art, and this activity will assist students in proving it.

➤ Use 12-by-18-inch posterboard to make an art palette pattern, and allow students to trace it to make their own palette.

➤ Students should divide the palette into four sections, and each section will contain a seasonal poem and illustration.

➤ In addition, students may wish to create another palette portraying seasonal poems they have written themselves, along with illustrations. Refer to the poetry section in Chapter 6.

Solar Jeopardy

1. Three-quarters of this element makes up the Sun.

    What is hydrogen?

2. To form this element, extremely high heat and hydrogen atoms join together.

    What is helium?

3. It is the distance from the Earth to the Sun.

    What is 93,000,000 miles?

4. It is twenty-eight times that of Earth's.

    What is the Sun's gravity?

5. Aurora borealis.

    What is caused when the solar wind collides with Earth's atmosphere at its poles?

6. Five billion years.

    How long will it be before the Sun uses up all its energy and becomes a red dwarf star?

7. 2,800 pounds.

    What would be your weight on the Sun if you weighed 100 pounds on Earth?

8. Solar wind.

    What are electrical charges that travel from the Sun at about 300 miles per second?

9. Sunspots.

    What are cooler, dark areas on the Sun?

10. Earth becomes a little warmer.

    What happens about every eleven years when there are many sunspots?

(Asimov, 1994)
(Darling, 1984)

Sun Questions

1. What is hydrogen?

   _____

2. What is helium?

   _____

3. What is 93,000,000 miles?

   _____

4. What is the Sun's gravity?

   _____

5. What is caused when the solar wind collides with Earth's atmosphere at its poles?

   _____

6. How long will it be before the Sun uses up all its energy and becomes a red dwarf star?

   _____

7. What would be your weight on the Sun if you weighed 100 pounds on Earth?

   _____

8. What are electrical charges that travel from the Sun at about 300 miles per second?

   _____

9. What are cooler, darker areas on the Sun?

   _____

10. What happens about every eleven years when there are many sunspots?

    _____

Frame Book

_____

_____

_____

_____

_____

_____

Solar Facts

Materials needed:
- worksheet with statements
- 12-by-18-inch construction paper
- glue
- sentence strips

Directions:
1. Below are eight statements based on the information your teacher has read from Seymour Simon's book *The Sun*. Not every statement is true.

2. Hold the construction paper lengthwise and write the title *Facts About the Sun* on the top of the paper.

3. Cut out each of the statements. If the statement is true, glue it onto the construction paper.

4. If the statement is not true, rewrite the statement on a sentence strip so that it is true, and then glue it onto the construction paper.

5. If you have room on the construction paper, add some illustrations.

Sun statements:
a. The Sun is a medium-sized star.
b. The Sun is much farther away from Earth than most stars.
c. Nuclear explosions within the Sun caused it to begin to shine.
d. Helium is what gives the Sun its energy.
e. Asteroids, planets, and comets orbit the Sun.
f. The Sun is so large, it could hold over one million Earths within it.
g. The Sun burns the way all fires do.
h. The Sun has so much hydrogen, that it will probably shine for five billion more years.

Parts of the Sun

Name _____ Date _____

Part I: Match the definition for each part of the Sun.

1. core _____

2. radiative zone _____

3. convective zone _____

4. photosphere _____

5. corona _____

6. chromosphere _____

a. a halo of light seen around the Sun during a solar eclipse

b. part of the Sun's atmosphere, seen as a pinkish color during a solar eclipse

c. center of the Sun; radiation is produced here.

d. an inner area of the Sun that helps move energy from the core to the atmosphere (closer to the photosphere)

e. the Sun's surface

f. an area that helps move energy away from the core of the Sun to its atmosphere (closer to the core)

Part II: Making your own Sun.

Materials needed for each group:
- a large Styrofoam ball
- a ring of white Styrofoam
- tempera paint: orange, yellow, white, black, red (mix with white to make pink for the chromosphere)
- toothpicks
- 3-by-3-inch yellow sticky notes
- an X-ACTO knife, to be used only by a teacher or other supervising adult

Directions:
a. An area of the Styrofoam ball should be cut away to show the inner area of the Sun.

b. With a pencil or marker, outline each part of the Sun. (See the cut-away picture of the parts of the Sun in Simon's book.)

c. Paint each section with the appropriate color.

d. Draw a line all the way around the white ring so that half of the ring will represent the corona, and the other half will represent the chromosphere. Paint the chromosphere pink.

e. Label each part by making a flag with the toothpicks and sticky notes.

f. After reading the next section of *The Sun*, you may want to add a prominence, a flare, and a sunspot to your Sun. Use black paint for sunspots and pipe cleaners or pieces of clay for prominences and flares.

g. Display the Sun models throughout the classroom and refer to them throughout the unit.

(Simon, 1989)

Sunrise/Sunset Time

Sample Page
October 1997

October 3

Sunrise: 6:58 A.M.   Sunset: 6:39 P.M.

Difference from September 26: 17 minutes

October 10

Sunrise: 7:05 A.M.   Sunset: 6:28 P.M.

Difference from October 3: 18 minutes

October 17

Sunrise: 7:13 A.M.   Sunset: 6:18 P.M.

Difference from October 10: 18 minutes

October 24

Sunrise: 7:20 A.M.   Sunset: 6:08 P.M.

Difference from October 17: 17 minutes

October 31 (Change from Daylight Savings Time to Eastern Standard Time)

Sunrise: 6:28 A.M.   Sunset: 4:59 P.M.

Difference from October 24: 17 minutes

Total difference in daylight time from September to October:
87 minutes (1 hour and 27 minutes).

Sunshape

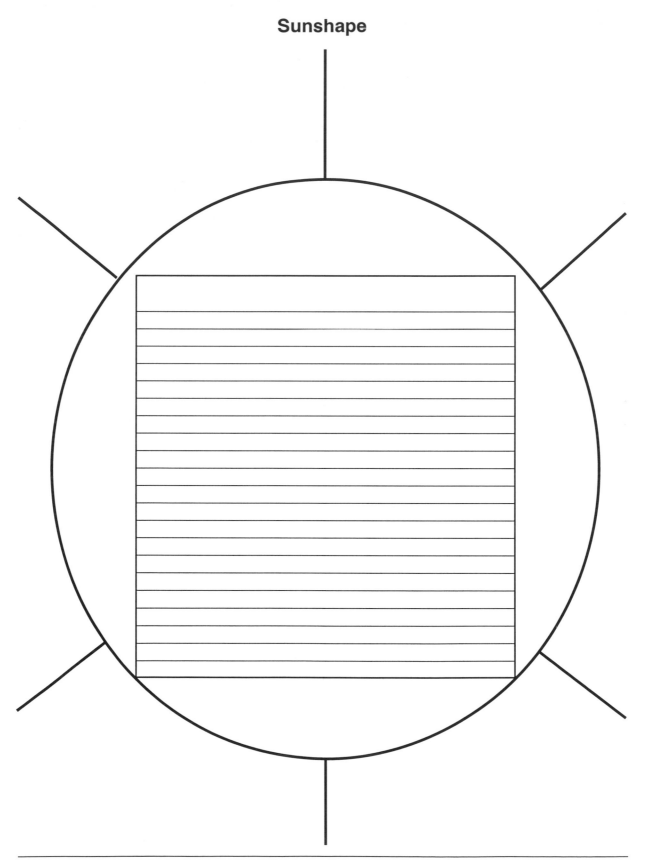

Sunpainters: Eclipse of the Navajo Sun

Name _____ Date _____

Prereading

1. List the colors of the rainbow:

    _____

2. For each color of the rainbow, name an item in nature that matches that color.

    _____

    _____

    _____

    _____

    _____

    _____

    _____

Remember as we read this story that the colors of the rainbow are contained in the light of the Sun. We will be learning more about rainbows soon.

During Reading

1. How would you feel if someone told you that the Sun had died?

    _____

    _____

2. What do you think would be a consequence of the death of the Sun?

    _____

    _____

3. What are some things you have learned about Navajo homes and food as you listen to the story?

    _____

    _____

4. Why do you think grandfather prays during the eclipse?

    _____

    _____

5. Why do you think it is important for Kii not to eat or drink during the eclipse?

    _____

    _____

Postreading

1. What does Kii do before finally eating? Why do you think he did these things?

    _____

    _____

    _____

2. What did you find out about the effect of a solar eclipse on Earth?

    _____

    _____

    _____

3. Why do you think nature, and what happens in nature, is so important to the Navajo people?

    _____

    _____

    _____

Solar Eclipse Brainstorming

Name _____ Date _____

Review: Moon Phases
              Lunar Eclipse Occurrence

1. Based on what you know of Moon phases and how a lunar eclipse occurs, during what
    Moon phase do you think a solar eclipse would occur?

    _____

2. Using the information you have about lunar eclipses, which celestial body, the Sun, Moon,
    or Earth, casts a shadow during a solar eclipse?

    _____

3. During a solar eclipse, a shadow would be cast upon which celestial body?

    _____

4. Illustrate your idea of how a solar eclipse occurs.

5. Save this sheet.

Solar Eclipse Science

Name _____ Date _____

1. A solar eclipse takes place during what Moon phase? _____

2. The _____ moves in front of the _____ during a solar eclipse.

3. The _____ casts a shadow on the _____ during a solar eclipse.

4. Illustrate a solar eclipse. Label all celestial bodies.

5. Define the following vocabulary words that one may use during a solar eclipse.
   a. Baily's beads _____
   b. corona _____
   c. penumbra _____
   d. total solar eclipse _____
   e. annular solar eclipse _____
   f. partial solar eclipse _____

Solar Eclipse Vocabulary

1. **Annular Eclipse**. A solar eclipse that is not total. The Moon is too far away from Earth to completely block out the Sun as the Earth, Moon, and Sun line up. A ring of the photosphere remains observable, and the corona cannot be seen.

2. **Baily's Beads**. During a solar eclipse, Baily's beads are observed just before the Moon blocks the Sun completely. It is the final bit of glowing Sun that appears as brightly jeweled beads. This occurs because the Sun's rays are being scattered by the landforms on the edge of the Moon. Sometimes there is a smaller eruption of light, known as the **diamond ring effect**.

3. **Corona**. The outermost layer of the Sun that can only be seen during a total solar eclipse.

4. **Partial Eclipse**. Only a part of the Moon covers the Sun. The Sun, Moon, and Earth do not line up completely.

5. **Path of Totality**. A small region on Earth, usually less than 100 miles wide, from which a total solar eclipse can be viewed.

6. **Penumbra**. A portion of a shadow.

7. **Solar Eclipse**. When the Earth, Moon, and Sun line up, and the Moon moves between the Sun and the Earth. This occurs only during the New Moon phase.

8. **Total Eclipse**. When the Moon completely blocks the Sun, allowing no light to reach Earth for a very short period of time.

(Aronson, 1996)
(Mitton, 1991)
(Snowden, 1990)

Discovering White Light

Name _____ Date _____

Prisms and Rainbows

1. When I look through the prism, I see:

    _____

    _____

2. When I spin the rainbow circle, I notice:

    _____

    _____

3. I think this happens because:

    _____

    _____

Diffraction Grating

1. When the diffraction grating is placed in front of the white light, I see:

    _____

    _____

    _____

2. I think this happens because:

    _____

    _____

    _____

White Light and Rainbows

1. These are some times when I have seen rainbows:

    _____

    _____

    _____

    _____

2. Based on the activities we have done, I think white light and rainbows have something in common because:

    _____

    _____

    _____

3. I know of some other ways to make rainbows:

    _____

    _____

    _____

    _____

Illustrations

Annotated Bibliography

Aronson, Billy. *Eclipses: Nature's Blackouts.* New York: Grolier, 1996.
Good introduction to the subject of solar and lunar eclipses. Includes photographs, a glossary, and simple scientific explanations.

Asimov, Isaac. *The Sun and Its Secrets.* Milwaukee, WI: Gareth Stevens, 1994.
A good resource for students in grades 4–6.

Berger, Melvin. *Wonders of Science.* New York: Scholastic, 1991.

Branley, Franklyn M. *Eclipse: Darkness in Daytime.* New York: Harper & Row, 1988.
A primary picture book with very simple descriptions of a solar eclipse.

Burns, George. *Exploring the World of Astronomy.* New York: Franklin Watts, 1995.
A book dealing with the Sun, Moon, and Stars, full of simple attractive photographs and simple science ideas for children.

Cheung, Euphine, and Tony Guo. *Er-Lang and the Suns.* New York: Mondo, 1994.
A Chinese folktale explaining how night and day came about.

Daly, Niki. *Why the Sun & Moon Live in the Sky.* New York: William Morrow, 1995.

Darling, David J. *The Sun: Our Neighborhood Star.* Minneapolis, MN: Dillon Press, 1984.
A good resource for middle elementary students.

d'Aulaire, Ingri, and Edgar Parin d'Aulaire. *d'Aulaires' Book of Greek Myths.* New York: Doubleday, 1962.

de Regniers, Beatrice Schenk, et al., comps. *Sing a Song of Popcorn.* New York: Scholastic, 1988.
Another excellent resource for poetry dealing with nature.

"Eclipse." *Odyssey* (July/August 1991).
Several articles contain information concerning the concept of a solar eclipse and how to make a solar viewer.

Gibbons, Gail. *The Reasons for the Seasons.* New York: Holiday House, 1995.
A simple picture book explaining how and why the seasons occur. Delightful illustrations and easy to understand.

Hadley, Eric, and Tessa Hadley. *Legends of the Sun and Moon.* Cambridge, MA: Cambridge University Press, 1983.
Short, two-page stories that retell legends from various parts of the world about the Sun and the Moon.

Horowitz, Anthony. *Myths and Legends.* New York: Kingfisher Books, 1994.
A teacher resource for various myths and legends around the world.

Low, Alice. *The Macmillan Book of Greek Gods and Heroes.* New York: Macmillan, 1985.
Retells simply many of the major Greek myths.

Milford, Susan. *Tales of the Shimmering Sky.* Charlotte, NC: Williamson, 1996.
An outstanding children's book recounting various tales of the sky's natures; includes a wide range of hands-on activities.

O'Neil, Mary. *Hailstones and Halibut Bones.* New York: Doubleday, 1961.
A wonderful book of poems about color; it is perfect to use with lessons on imagery, rainbows, and light. It is still in print, available in paperback.

Osborne, Mary Pope. *Favorite Greek Myths.* New York: Scholastic, 1989.
Although this book retells some of the most popular Greek myths in a delightful way, be aware that the corresponding Roman names are used rather than the Greek names.

Pearce, Q. L. *Lightning and Other Wonders of the Sky.* Englewood Cliffs, NJ: RGA, 1989.

This book relates, in simple, narrative terms, the various sky phenomena that take place.

Pfister, Marcus. *Sun and Moon*. New York: Scholastic, 1990.
The story of a solar eclipse and friendship between the Sun and the Moon.

Prelutsky, Jack, comp. *The Random House Book of Poetry*. New York: Random House, 1983.
This poetry anthology contains delightful nature poems.

Ruiz, Andres Llamas. *Seasons*. New York: Sterling, 1996.
This book explains, month by month, what takes place seasonally during the month and illustrates Earth's position in relation to the Sun.

Simon, Seymour. *The Sun*. New York: William Morrow, 1989.
A book containing NASA photographs and simple facts about the Sun, its composition, and its behavior.

Snowden, Sheila. *The Young Astronomer*. Tulsa, OK: EDC, 1990.
An excellent resource for students and teachers with respect to all astronomy topics.

Whitehorne, Baje. *Sunpainters: Eclipse of the Navajo Sun*. Flagstaff, AZ: Northland, 1994.
A Navajo tale that takes place during a solar eclipse.

References and Resources

Bondurant, Lynn R. Jr. *Touching Tomorrow: The Sun Part I and II*. Cleveland, OH: NASA and Educational TV, 1991.
Activities related to the Sun, shadows, and time-keeping.

Branley, Franklyn M. *Keeping Time*. Boston: Houghton Mifflin, 1993.
Describes all different types of time, how and why it occurs, and hands-on activities.

——. *Sun Dogs and Shooting Stars: A Skywatcher's Guide*. New York: Avon Books, 1980.
Details of what can be found in the sky during each month of the year along with a variety of easy, hands-on activities.

Carey, Patsy, Cynthia Holzschuber, and Susan Kilpatrick. *Activities for Any Literature Unit*. Huntington Beach, CA: Teacher Created Materials, 1995.
A wonderful resource for literature-based activities.

Mecham, Karen Hales. *Space Exploration: Primary Science Resource Guide*. St. Louis, MO: Milliken, 1992.
Contains an excellent poster of the parts of the Sun and Earth's revolution around the Sun.

Mitton, Jacqueline. *Dictionary of Astronomy*. London: Penguin Books, 1991.
A teacher resource for astronomy vocabulary.

Sears, Peter. *Gonna Bake Me a Rainbow Poem*. New York: Scholastic, 1990.
In addition to publishing a variety of poetry written by students, this book imparts suggestions for teaching students how to write poetry.

VanCleave, Janice. *Astronomy for Every Kid*. New York: John Wiley, 1991.
Simple science experiments for all astronomy subtopics.

Vogt, Gregory L. *Space-Based Astronomy: Teacher's Guide with Activities*. Washington, DC: NASA, 1994.
All types of experiments, dealing with light, color, and telescopes; some will need to be adapted for younger students.

Young Astronaut Program. *Making a Sundial*. Vol. 6: *Ulysses: A New View of the Sun*. Washington, DC: Young Astronaut Council, 1990.

——. *Reasons for the Seasons*. Vol. 6: *At Home in the Universe*. Washington, DC: Young Astronaut Council, 1991.

Musical Resources

Buchman, Rachel. *Sing a Song of Seasons.* Cambridge, MA: Rounder Records, 1997.
Folk songs covering all four seasons, geared toward primary students.

Electronic Sources

Berger, Michael. 1997. *The Virtual Tour of the Sun.* 1996. URL: http://www.astro.uva.nl/michielb/od95 (Accessed June 26, 1997).
A great way to "observe" the Sun through photographs.

Charboneau, P., and O. R. White. 1995. *The Sun: A Pictorial Introduction.* URL: http://www.hao.ucar.edu/public/slides/slides.html (Accessed June 26, 1997).
A variety of solar photos along with detailed descriptions.

Charles, Jeffrey. 1997. *The Eclipse Chaser-Guide to WOW.* URL: http://www.eclipsechaser.com (Accessed June 27, 1997).
Photos and information about solar eclipses.

Espenak, Fred. Fred Espenak's *Eclipse Home Page.* URL: http://sunearth.gsfc.nasa.gov/eclipse/eclipse.html (Accessed July 22, 1997).
Photos and information about solar and lunar eclipses.

Lynds, Beverly T. 1997. *About Rainbows.* URL: http://www.unidata.ucar.edu/staff/blynds/rnbw.html (Accessed September 15, 1997).
Explanation of what a rainbow is and how it is formed. Has links to other sites.

SkyPublishingCorporation. 1997. *Skyonline Eclipse Page.* URL: http://www.skypub.com/eclipses/eclipses.shtml (Accessed June 27, 1997).
Photos and information about lunar and solar eclipses.

Stern, Fred. 1997. *Rainbow Maker Home Page.* URL: http://www.zianet.com/rainbowhome.htm (Accessed July 1, 1997).
Rainbow information and photographs.

United States Navy. 1996. *Data Services.* URL: http://aa.usno.navy.mil/AA/data (Accessed August 13, 1997).
Gives information about sunrise/sunset times in specific locations.

Wang, Randy. 1997. *Rainbows by Randy Wang.* URL: http://http.cs.berkeley.edu/~rywang/magic_small/rainbows.html (Accessed July 1, 1997).
Rainbow haiku and photographs.

CHAPTER 3

The Planets

Introduction

Before starting a unit on the planets, contact your local TRC for NASA photographs of each of the planets and display them around the room, labeled only with the name. Prior to reading any of the stories described below, give students a chance to scrutinize these photographs over a period of a few days and record some of their thoughts and observations about each planet, using a chart or worksheet entitled, "My First Impressions of the Planets." To enhance this activity and strengthen vocabulary skills, include the use of "Planetary Adjectives" (see pages 72–73). After completing the worksheet, have students write descriptive paragraphs or various types of sentences using the adjectives and synonyms. Refer to these assignments when discussing the origin of the planet names or when researching any of the planets.

Literature and the Planets

The Greek creation myth, *My Place in Space*, or *The Magic School Bus Lost in the Solar System* are three pieces of literature that can be used to introduce the planets to students. Following are some suggestions for using these three stories.

The Greek Creation Myth: The Story of the Titans

The Greek creation myth can be found in most mythology books. Two possibilities include *The Macmillan Book of Greek Gods and Heroes* or *d'Aulaires' Book of Greek Myths*. The stories describe the Titans as the first gods, with Zeus eventually becoming the king of the gods, and his brothers and offspring becoming some of the most important gods. Many of the corresponding Roman names from these myths were later used to name celestial objects. Try the following to interest students in learning the names of the planets and the names' origins.

1. Read aloud one of the two stories from the mythology books mentioned. Because the creation myth's cast of characters and events can become confusing, allow students to jot down some notes using the reproducible "A Family of Planets" (see page 74). Due to the length and the amount of information involved, allow at least two days for the reading of the story.

2. Review information on the worksheet and have students work in small groups to create a family tree that indicates how all the planet names are related to Zeus (Jupiter).

3. See the outline of the example of one family tree idea (below), which uses construction paper to make the planets, yarn to make the connections, and large, stick-on labels to name each planet and its relationship to Jupiter. Give students some freedom in devising ways to create the family tree and show the connections. I have had students create their own mobiles to demonstrate their understanding of the planets and their names. Students may also make trees using real tree branches as connections to leaves, which indicate the planet names.

4. Students should use their listening worksheet and any other resource books available to assist them. Be sure that students understand that, although the names of the planets are connected to Jupiter, *all* the planets revolve around the Sun. See *Astronomy Today* for an excellent illustration of the revolution of the planets around the Sun.

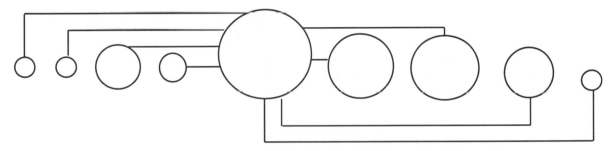

The Planet Family
Curved line = Sun; Mercury, the messenger and quickest god = Jupiter's son; Venus, the goddess of love was born of the sea, but cared for by Jupiter; Earth or Gaea = Jupiter's grandmother; Mars, the red planet and the god of war = Jupiter's brother; Jupiter, the largest planet = the king of Gods; Saturn = Jupiter's father; Uranus = Jupiter's grandfather; Neptune, the blue planet and god of the sea = Jupiter's brother; Pluto, the coldest planet and god of the underworld = Jupiter's brother.

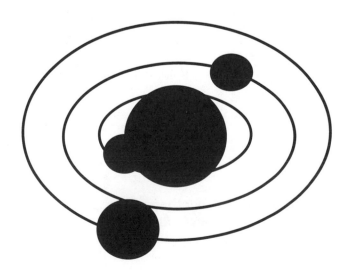

As you continue researching and studying the planets, you will find that, in most cases, the satellites or moons of each planet have names that are mythologically related to each individual planet.

A Bus in the Solar System

Most primary students are already familiar with Mrs. Frizzle and her scientific adventures in the *Magic School Bus*, so you may want to come to school one day dressed as Mrs. Frizzle, or have a willing student take on her role, to introduce a learning center using the *Lost in the Solar System* book and the audiotape that goes with it. The information in this book relies on information gained from the Voyager and other NASA planetary missions in the 1970s and 1980s, and even as this book is being written, new information on the planets continues to be acquired. However, the basics are fairly constant, and as the unit of study proceeds, research by students will add current information. Consider the following suggestions to set up the center. You will need an audiotape player that has connections for at least four headsets.

1. Display the NASA photographs of each planet, and have three or four books available so that students may follow along as they listen to the tape.

2. Have accessible pencils and the worksheet entitled, "Lost in the Solar System," for students to complete as they read the book and listen to the tape. The worksheet should have a place for students to record facts about each planet and questions they may have.

3. Students are always interested in their weight on different planets, so instruct students how to use calculators and the "Gravity Factor Chart" reproducible (see page 75), to compute and graph their weight on each planet and Earth's Moon. Place the needed materials for this activity at the center.

4. When students have completed these activities, have them make a T-shaped booklet, adapted from *Using Nonfiction Effectively in Your Classroom*.

    *   From construction paper, students should cut out twelve (nine for planets, one for asteroids, one for a cover, and one for a conclusion) T-shapes using the "T-Shape" pattern reproducible on page 59. Students may want to use different colors for each T-shape, such as blue for Neptune or red for Mars.

    *   In the middle of each T-shape, students should place the name of the planet along with an illustration, and each of the four sides should contain facts about the planet (illustrations, if desired) based on information gathered from the *Magic School Bus*.

    *   Use one of the last two T-shapes to create a cover for the booklet, and in the middle box of the last T-shape, students should state which planet they would most like to visit, or would like to learn more about. Each box around the middle should state why the student would most like to visit this planet or questions students may have about it.

    *   Gather all the T-shapes together and staple at the top to bind the booklet.

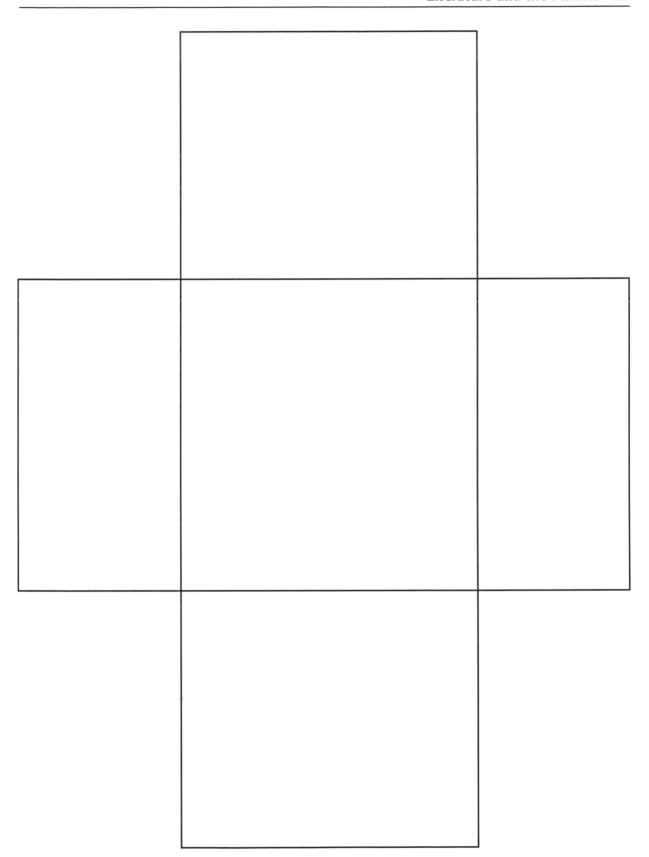

What Did You Say Your Address Was?

My Place in Space is a good, overall introduction to astronomy, because it will lead to questions about light years and galaxies, not just the planets. It is also a festive first-day-of-school activity because it provides a way for you and the new class to get to know one another. If you are not planning on studying astronomy as the school year begins, save the cards the students complete for later in the year.

Begin by asking students to write their addresses on a 3-by-5-inch index card, and when they are finished, read the addresses aloud. Ask students if they are sure that they are correct, and let them know that after reading *My Place in Space*, they may want to change their address cards. If you can, obtain several copies of the story, so that students may read together in small groups or at least follow along as you read aloud, enabling everyone to view the illustrations. At the completion of the story reading, students are almost certain to want to revise their address cards. Do this in any of the following ways.

1. Ahead of time, prepare a card for each student by placing a 5-by-8-inch index card at the top of a piece of 9-by-12-inch posterboard, leaving the bottom available for illustrations. Students may then write their new address on the index card.

2. Students may wish to use the classroom computer(s) by writing their new address in different fonts and using color and graphics, if available.

3. Turn this into a letter-writing lesson by having students write and illustrate a letter, using their new addresses, to a grandparent or other special person.

4. When all is said and done, send a few students to the school secretary with a list of new addresses for all the students in the class, and let her know that all the data in the computer will need to be changed. (Won't she be thrilled?)

5. If this is a first-day-of-school activity, take a few minutes to have students walk around the room, shake hands with classmates, and introduce themselves using their new addresses.

6. If it is not the first day of school, students can pretend that they are meeting one another for the first time, or one person could assume the role of Mrs. Frizzle, and students could introduce themselves to her as they board the bus and continue the exploration of their places in space.

7. In addition, if you completed the T-shape activity, another T-shape could be added with each student's new address.

8. As a homework assignment, instruct students to tell their parents that evening that they learned to write their address in school that day, tell their parents what it is, and have family members write their new addresses as well.

An additional activity that corresponds with *My Place in Space* can be found in *At Home in the Universe*, a Young Astronaut activity from the May/June 1991 booklet.

Planetary Math

Before studying each individual planet, practice mathematical calculations by creating a scale model of the Sun-planet system.

1. The following materials will be needed:

    *   A piece of black butcher paper, at least four feet long and two feet wide.

    *   Construction paper of various colors to represent each planet.

    *   Scissors and glue.

    *   "Scale Diameter Chart of the Planets" and "Planet Distance from the Sun" reproducibles (see pages 76 and 77).

    *   Tape measures, rulers, compasses, calculators, and 3-by-5-inch index cards.

2. Have students determine the scale diameter of each planet and its distance from the Sun using the reproducibles.

3. On the left side of the butcher paper, draw the Sun in a curved shape from the top of the paper to the bottom. It is difficult to make the Sun to scale because it is about 100 times the size of Earth.

4. Make each planet from construction paper using the diameter calculated and place it in its proper position and distance from the Sun on the butcher paper.

5. Use the index cards to label each planet, including a fact about the planet and its name origin.

Planet Trekking

You can organize a study of the planets in a number of ways for an entire class. Consider having all students read each of the myths that correspond with the planet names, complete a choice of literature responses, and then concentrate their research on just one planet. Another possibility, for small groups of students to focus on just one planet, would include: reading just the one myth based on that planet's name; using a literature response activity to retell the myth so all students would become familiar; and completing a research project. Suggestions for fact and fiction reading, literature responses, hands-on activities, and research are included in this segment of the chapter. Choose from any of these activities, mix and match, and adapt to the needs and abilities of your class.

Planet Facts

Using any of the Seymour Simon or Gregory Vogt planet books, create a list of questions whose answers are facts about each planet or comets and asteroids. Consider this idea:

> ➤ Once a week, take one of the planet question sheets and write each question on a sentence strip.

> ➤ Display the sentence strips around the room and have fact books on the planets available for students' use.

> ➤ During time periods that you specify, students should read to find the answers to the questions, and record their responses.

> ➤ At the end of the week (or every two or three days, if you prefer), discuss the responses, and continue the same process the following week.

Fiction/Fact Reading

Each planet's individual myth can be found in *d'Aulaires' Book of Greek Myths*, but be sure to remember to apply the corresponding Roman name. Excerpts with regard to each planet's corresponding myth can be found in *The Macmillan Book of Greek Gods and Heroes*, *The Olympians*, and at the website *Windows to the Universe*, http://www.windows.umich. edu as of July 13, 1997. A very interesting African legend that explains the appearance of Venus in the east in the morning and in the west during the evening is *The Orphan Boy*.

Factual readings of the planets can be put together using several sources named in the bibliography following this chapter, as well as numerous websites. Although fact books will be used more during the research process, you may wish to charge students with the task of completing both a fictional and factual reading, executing a literature response or combination of responses for both types of literature. Some students may be interested in reading fact books about asteroids or comets, as well.

Literature Responses

Most of the suggested literature response activities, with some adaptations, can be used for both nonfiction and fiction reading.

Sentence-Strip Chart. Have students retell any of the myths by writing main events, in sequence, on sentence strips, and secure the strips on a large piece of chart paper. Illustrations may be added, and the chart can be displayed for everyone to read.

Acrostic Poetry. Acrostic poetry lists the name of an object, in this case, the planet, vertically, and a sentence or phrase about that object is written next to each of the letters in the name of the object. Each poem line must be written beginning with the letter in the name of the object, and illustrations may be added. See the example below. This would be a good exercise for word processing practice also. Students can use different fonts, colors, and graphics to enhance their work.

 ercury is the planet closest to the Sun.

 ighty-eight days equals one Mercury year.

 idges and fractures on Mercury are like wrinkled apples.

 raters on Mercury are all different sizes.

 nless it is twilight or just before sunset, Mercury's brightness makes it difficult to see.

 oman god, Mercury, is where this planet got its name.

 ou would be very uncomfortable on Mercury because of its extreme cold and extreme heat.

Acrostic Poetry Example.

Book Jacket. Recycle paper grocery bags by making them into jackets for students to wear. Cut the bags up the middle to create an opening for the jacket, and then an armhole on either side, so that a student will be able to wear the jacket when it is ready to be exhibited. Place the name of the planet on the jacket and decorate the jacket with various pictures and/or objects that represent facts about the planet, some aspect of its myth, or both.

Windsock. Use construction paper or posterboard to create the top of the windsock, which will represent the planet. From this rounded piece, hang tissue paper strips and attach facts or story parts, written on index cards.

Questions and Answers. Have students devise their own Jeopardy-type game or crossword puzzle based on planet facts and/or planet myths.

Postcards. Students may wish to design a variety of picture postcards that depict either the facts about the planet or some of the mythological events. Use 5-by-8-inch index cards for this activity, with the blank side for pictures, and a sentence or two on the back left-hand corner to describe the illustration. A set of stamps for the planet may also be designed to go along with the postcards.

Tactile Activities

Although several of the previous projects could be considered hands-on, the following suggestions specifically target tactile skills.

➤ Salt-Dough Planets

For this project, students make a model of one of the planets using salt dough. I generally make the salt dough right in the classroom on the day it is to be used; however, it can be made ahead of time and kept tightly sealed in a plastic bag to keep it soft. Once it is removed from the bag, however, it should be used right away. The dough is soft and pliable, making it easy for students to create various features, such as craters, ridges, mountains, etc., that are found on the planets.

RECIPE FOR SALT DOUGH

two cups of flour   one cup of water
one cup of salt

Blend all ingredients together in a bowl so that you have a pliable clay and use right away. It will be sticky.

Other Materials Needed

a square piece of foamboard, about 9 by 9 inches, for each group
tempera paint and paintbrushes
Popsicle sticks
paper towels
water

compasses for circle drawing
X-ACTO knife (teacher use only)
small bowl for each group in which to place salt dough

Foamboard can be found in most arts and crafts stores and comes in large sheets that can be easily cut into squares with an X-ACTO knife. The salt dough recipe will give you enough dough for two to three planets. It is a messy project, so be prepared, and advise students not to eat the salt dough, mostly due to its very high salt content. Follow these directions for making the salt dough planets. X-ACTO knife is for teacher use only. Do not allow students to handle the knife.

1. Have each group of students decide which planet they will re-create, and first illustrate it on paper. Be sure to include as many of the planet features as possible.

2. On the foamboard, students should use the compass to draw a circle that would represent the approximate size of the planet. You may want to use larger pieces of foamboard for the larger planets.

3. Give students a container of salt dough and have them begin placing it on the foamboard to form the shape of the planet. Using their hands and Popsicle sticks, they can create the various planet features.

4. Let the planets dry overnight and paint them the next day.

5. Display along with other projects or with planet research reports.

➤ Planet Patterns

This next activity is a little less messy, but just as much fun and probably easier for younger students. Students should use plain fabric that has the basic background color of the planet and a variety of natural materials such as pasta shapes, beans, peas, small seashells, small, plain aquarium stone, pieces of rice or cereal, coconut, etc. The fabric, cut in a circular shape, should be placed on posterboard or foamboard. Students may then use the natural materials to re-create the features of the planets, and may also use fabric paint or crayons to note ridges, fractures, dried waterbeds, or other features for which the natural materials do not work well.

➤ Other Solar System Activities

There are several other planetary hands-on activities that can be found in a variety of editions of Young Astronaut lessons. *Voyager: The Grand Tour* covers the mission of the space probe Voyager II to the planets Jupiter, Saturn, Uranus, and Neptune during the 1980s. This comes with a videotape as well. The 1993 Teacher's Resource edition includes scale models of the solar system, an activity that emphasizes Saturn's rings and an activity that models the shapes (not completely round) of Jupiter and Saturn.

For a study of Jupiter, use the 1989 Young Astronaut packet *Galileo to Jupiter*, and the 1995 Galileo program published by the Outreach Department at the Jet Propulsion Laboratory. For the most up-to-date information on Jupiter and four of its moons that the space probe Galileo is studying, visit this website: http://www.jpl.nasa.gov/galileo (as of July 12, 1997).

An investigation of Mars could include excellent activities found in two Young Astronaut packets, *Return to Mars* and *Mission to Mars*. You will find activities for watching Mars in the night sky, studying its two moons, Phobos and Deimos, observing its features, and making a model of Mars so that it really is red. *Nergal, the 4th Planet: An Exercise in Imagination* is an elementary activity book designed and published by NASA that benefits a study of Mars. Investigate the websites *Mars Global Surveyor* at http://mgs-www.jpl.nasa.gov and *Mars Pathfinder Mission* at http://mpfwww.arc.nasa.gov (as of July 13, 1997).

➤ *A Space Probe Landing*

Because NASA sends many space probes to planets, the following activity allows students to think about how a space probe lands on a hard-surface planet, such as Mars or Mercury, without crushing. In this experiment, students will prepare a box so that when the box is dropped from an elevated height, its contents, which will be a raw egg, will not break.

Egg Drop

1. Divide the class into small groups, and give each group the same type and size box, which will be considered the landing craft.

2. Charge students with the task of designing the box so that it will land on Mercury or Mars with the space probe (the egg) intact.

3. Decide on other basic directions, such as whether you will supply choices of materials for packing, allow students to bring things from home, or a combination of both.

4. Decide also whether you will permit items such as parachutes and balloons, or whether the egg may be encased inside another type of material other than the box. All space probe protection should be inside the box, not outside.

5. The landing craft and space probe may be given names; the landing craft may be decorated, and patches may be designed for this mission. (NASA sanctions patches for all space missions, manned or unmanned. See Chapter 5 for information on mission patches.)

6. Once students are satisfied with their landing craft, the egg should be placed inside the box, and the box should be securely taped.

7. Locate an area that is at least ten feet off the ground, and allow either students, if it is safe for them, or an adult (I ask our school custodian to drop the boxes from the roof of the school) to drop the landing craft boxes.

8. Students may observe from a safe distance, if they are not dropping the boxes, and retrieve them after all have landed.

9. Return to the classroom to investigate the contents of the landing craft and evaluate using the reproducible "Egg Drop Experiment" (see pages 78–79).

Planets and Prose

➤ *A Creature in the Cupboard*

Several planet activities thus far have focused on scientific facts. Because students *know* that aliens really do exist, proposing a creative writing assignment about creatures from other planets is certain to produce interest. If students are familiar with the novel *The Indian in the Cupboard*, suggest that they will be forming their own planetary creature that will be small enough to bring to school with them. Consider the following suggestions.

1. To start students thinking, tell them that their planetary creature will be from the planet they researched, so it is important that their creature be structured to represent that planet in some way. For homework that night, students should begin to contemplate ideas about their creature's appearance.

2. The following day, have several different colors of modeling clay available.

3. Give students a small paper plate, along with the colors of clay they have chosen, and allow about forty-five minutes to create their space creature.

4. The space creature may be named and set aside until the following day, when students should have the opportunity to add or make changes to their creatures.

5. Once students have completed their space creatures, ask them to complete the reproducible "Space Creature Writing Web" (see pages 80–81). Sometimes students enjoy including some of their classmates' space creatures in their stories as additional characters.

6. Decide what area of writing, such as humor, dialogue, paragraphing, description, fairy tale, tall tale, etc., you may wish to highlight in this assignment. I often ask students to concentrate on dialogue writing in this assignment, with a special emphasis on speaker-tag vocabulary. I also caution students to beware of getting too carried away with exaggeration and/or including violent situations.

7. Students should proceed through the writing process, and share and display their stories and space creatures when complete.

➤ *Beyond Cupboard Creatures*

Other possible space creature writing activities include:

➤ How-to paragraphs explaining how to do something on Earth, such as riding a bicycle, with which the space creature may not be familiar.

➤ A vacation, camping, or weekend outing with family that could include comparison and contrast of the physical features of the creature's home planet and the vacation site.

➤ Continuing with the idea of taking a trip, prepare for the journey with the space creature. Have students respond to questions such as: What new clothes will you or the space creature need? What other preparations will you and your space creature need to make for this adventure?

> ➤   Write a journal entry from the space creature's view upon its first sighting at this new spot on Earth, and include some vocabulary from the space creature's language.

Whatever you and your class decide to do with space creature or creative writing, learn from it and have a good time, too!

Asteroids and Comets

Studying planets should also include some investigation of asteroids and comets. Although asteroids are found orbiting the Sun in various places throughout the solar system, many are found inside the asteroid belt between Mars and Jupiter. Specific asteroids have been named and examined by some of the unmanned space probes sent to explore planets, and comets have been studied for years by astronomers. If the class studies dinosaurs at any time, an in-depth look at asteroids may be warranted because more theories are being advanced regarding the relationship between the extinction of dinosaurs and asteroids.

Refer to the chapter bibliography for comet and asteroid websites, as well as print materials for further study. Look for a wonderful demonstration activity, "How to Make a Comet," found in *Astro Adventures*; it really does work, and students are fascinated.

Mission to Planet Earth

Introduction

A study of Earth can encompass many areas, leading to the study of weather, water, the environment, pollution, and various biomes. This section focuses on certain areas of NASA's *Our Mission to Planet Earth* and a few simple ways in which your class can study Earth.

Begin by asking students to pretend they are traveling in space and viewing Earth from the space shuttle, approximately 200 miles above the atmosphere. Perhaps some students have flown in airplanes, although the view isn't quite the same. What do they see as they orbit the Earth? Prompt students to draw, and then paint, using watercolors, their view of Earth from outer space. Once students have completed this task, share NASA photographs that have been taken from space. The photographs can be ordered from your regional NASA TRC or found in Patricia Lauber's *Seeing Earth from Space*. Compare and contrast students' pictures with the photographs and discuss students' thoughts and impressions.

Because there are so many aspects to a study of Earth, students may want to choose a direction that specifically interests them. A particular social studies unit or class novel may lead you to study the rainforest, the desert, the ocean, etc. Following are suggestions and resources to assist in the exploration of the planet on which we live.

Literature and Planet Earth

The Greek myths and the legends from many different cultures continue to be excellent sources of fictional reading, the study of nature, and our own planet. Give students a chance to read several different tales and complete responses to literature. Notable Native American story suggestions are:

➢ *Between Earth and Sky*

➢ *Remaking the Earth*

➢ *Keepers of the Night*

➢ Stories found in *North American Indians: Myths and Legends*

Some Greek/Roman myths are:

➢ The story of the seasons involving Persephone, Demeter (Ceres), and Hades (Pluto)

➢ Pan, the Greek god of nature

➢ Eos, the mother of the four winds

➢ Prometheus, the giver of fire

➢ Deucalion, Prometheus's son, who survived a flood

Direct students to read a specified number of stories and choose from any of the following as a literature response:

1. Event Map Booklet. To do this, students should make one event map for each story that they read and bind the maps together in a booklet. Consider these directions for the event map.

   a. For each event map use a base piece of construction paper that is 12 by 18 inches, held horizontally.

   b. Each event map will include the beginning of the story, three major occurrences in the story, and the conclusion, all described in writing.

   c. Each item for the event map will be written on a separate cut-out piece of construction paper, and then placed on the base piece of construction paper.

   d. On all the event maps, the same color construction paper will be used for each of the beginnings, another color for all the occurrences, and a third color for all the conclusions.

   e. For any of the items, shapes may be cut out that represent a connection to the legend or myth.

   f. The title of the story should be written at the top of each event map, and small drawings may be added.

   g. See illustration on page 70. Instead of binding all the event maps together right away, save them and, after completing some of the Earth science activities from later in this chapter, add those to the booklet.

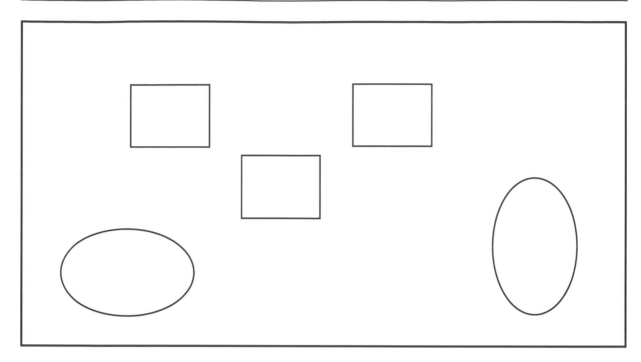

Event Map Format.

2. Sentence-Strip Chart. For each legend, give students five to six sentence strips, and have them write the major event from the story on each of the strips. Place the strips, in sequence, on a large piece of chart paper, illustrate, and display.

3. Scrapbook. Have students work with a partner to create a scrapbook based on any of the Earth myths and legends. Have each pair jot down six major occurrences in the story and plan how each occurrence could be portrayed in a still photograph. Students should then pose for each picture, taken with either a Polaroid camera or digital camera. The Polaroid photos may be arranged on posterboard with written captions and made into a scrapbook, or the digital camera photos can be arranged on the computer with written captions, printed, and compiled into a scrapbook.

Earth Poetry

Most assuredly, nature is one of the most popular topics for poems, especially those for children. Poems such as "I'm Glad the Sky Is Painted Blue," "The Universe," and "All Things Bright and Beautiful" certainly work well when discussing planet Earth, and can be found, along with many others, in *The Random House Book of Poetry for Children*. Read several poems with students and have them interpret them through dramatization, art, or music. To write their own poetry, have students make a list of favorite nature topics, and refer to the section on poetry in Chapter 6. Pattern poems and onomatopoeia poems work well with this topic.

Earth Science

NASA publishes an enormous number of lesson plans and background information through their Mission to Earth program. These materials can be requested from your regional TRC. Following are some suggestions and resources.

➤ *Our Mission to Planet Earth: A Guide to Teaching Earth System Science* is geared for grades K–3. Ask for the *Mission to Planet Earth* coloring book, too.

➤ For upper elementary students, request *Earth's Mysterious Atmosphere: Atlas 1 Teacher's Guide with Activities.* These lessons are geared for middle-school students, but can be adapted for grades 4 and 5, and include lessons on the greenhouse effect and the ozone layer.

➤ *Explore New Worlds Through Science and Technology* is an activity booklet published by the National Science Foundation and includes activities on water, recycling, and how to plan a birthday party for Earth.

➤ NASA has videos and activity packets available entitled, "Beyond the Clouds," which is a study of the upper atmosphere, and "The Atmosphere Below," which is a study of changes in Earth's atmosphere.

➤ Background sheets, on such topics as the ozone layer, the greenhouse effect, clouds, and the weather effects of El Niño, are also available from your regional TRC. Be sure to ask for the lithographs of Earth, many taken from various space shuttle missions, that NASA distributes.

➤ An IMAX film, *The Blue Planet,* is available on video, and the Office of Education at the National Air and Space Museum has a teaching packet to accompany the video.

➤ Scholastic publishes a theme packet called *Environments,* which includes a short story about the rainforest, a Cherokee legend, "The Legend of the Bluebonnet," and "Earth Songs," poems by Myra Cohn Livingston. The packet also contains response and science ideas for each book.

➤ Two *Odyssey* magazine editions devoted to Earth are "Getting Caught Up in Earth's Atmosphere" and "Biodiversity: Earth's Living Treasure."

➤ Young Astronaut activity guides that deal specifically with Earth are: *Our Fragile Future,* containing experiments with clouds, weather, and pollution; *Earth: A View from Space,* which includes activities on the effects of erosion, water, and ocean currents; *Earth Search, Part II,* which assists a study of Earth with experiments about water, life on Earth, the land, and the air; and *Biosphere 2,* which includes activities on the various biomes.

➤ *Weather* by Janice VanCleave and *Simple Weather Experiments with Everyday Materials* are also excellent sources of investigations regarding the phenomena that take place on Earth.

Studying the planets, with a focus on planet Earth, can be a wonderful learning and fascinating experience for students. I hope this chapter has given you a few good ideas to get you started.

Planetary Adjectives

Name _____ Date _____

Directions: Next to the name of each planet, write adjectives describing what you see in the planet photographs. Use a thesaurus or dictionary to help you find synonyms and/or antonyms for the adjectives you have selected.

Name of Planet	Adjective(s)	Synonym(s)	Antonym(s)
Mercury			
Venus			
Earth			
Mars			
Asteroids			

Name of Planet	Adjective(s)	Synonym(s)	Antonym(s)
Jupiter			
Saturn			
Uranus			
Neptune			
Pluto			
Comets			

From *Soaring Through the Universe*. © 1999 Joanne C. Letwinch. Teacher Ideas Press. (800) 237-6124.

A Family of Planets

Name _____ Date _____

Title of myth(s) read: _____

_____

As the creation myths are read, on the first line next to each character's name, write the part the character played in the legend and how he/she was related to one of the other characters.
    Example: **Uranus:** Father Heaven, husband of Gaea, father of Cronus.

On the second line, write why you think the story explains the fact that the planet was named after this mythological character. Think about what type of character each one portrays.
    Example: **Jupiter:** the largest planet, was king of the gods.

Gaea: _____

_____

Uranus: _____

_____

Cronus (Saturn):   _____

_____

**Rhea (One of Saturn's moons
is named for Rhea):**   _____

_____

Zeus (Jupiter):   _____

_____

Poseidon (Neptune):   _____

_____

Hades (Pluto):   _____

_____

Hermes (Mercury):   _____

_____

Ares (Mars):   _____

_____

Aphrodite (Venus):   _____

_____

Gravity Factor Chart

Name _____ Date _____

Name of Planet	Gravity Factor	My Weight on Earth	My Weight on This Planet
Mercury	.38		
Venus	.82		
Earth	1.0		
Mars	.38		
Jupiter	2.87		
Saturn	1.32		
Uranus	.93		
Neptune	1.23		
Pluto	.03		
Earth's Moon	.167		

Once you have calculated your weight on each planet, display the information on a bar graph.

(*Philadelphia Inquirer*, 1992)

Scale Diameter Chart of the Planets

Name _____   Date _____

Scale is in inches, with Earth equal to two inches in diameter. Multiply the planet's diameter by two to get the scale diameter of each planet.

Planet	In Comparison to Earth-Diameter of Planet	Scale Diameter of Planet
Mercury	0.4	
Venus	0.9	
Earth	1.0	2.0
Mars	0.5	
Jupiter	11.0	
Saturn	9.0	18.0
Uranus	4.0	
Neptune	4.0	
Pluto	0.2	

(*Philadelphia Inquirer*, 1992)

Planet Distance from the Sun

The distance of each planet from the Sun is measured in astronomical units (AU). Earth's distance from the Sun is 1 astronomical unit or 93,000,000 miles; Mercury's distance from the Sun is 0.4 astronomical units. Each planet's distance from the Sun, on a scale model, can be measured in inches (such as 1 inch for Earth and .4 inches for Mercury), centimeters, feet, or meters. A classroom model works better using inches or centimeters; an outdoor model is better with feet or meters.

Planet	Distance from Sun in Astronomical Units
Mercury	0.4
Venus	0.7
Earth	1.0
Mars	1.5
Jupiter	5.2
Saturn	9.5
Uranus	19.2
Neptune	30.1
Pluto	39.4

Note: Every 248 years, Pluto's orbit around the Sun takes it inside Neptune's for twenty years. Neptune will be the farthest planet from the Sun until 1999.

(*Philadelphia Inquirer*, 1992)

Egg Drop Experiment

Name _____

Date _____

1. The name of my group's space probe mission is _____

2. The name of our landing craft is _____

3. The name of our space probe is _____

4. The materials we used to design our landing craft and protect the space probe from damage are:

    _____

    _____

5. We chose these materials because:

    _____

    _____

6. The inside of our landing craft looks something like this:

7. We launched our landing craft and space probe on _____ (date), from a height of _____ , and it landed (without damage to the space probe/with damage to the space probe) _____ .

8. We think our space probe (survived/did not survive) its landing because:

    _____

    _____

    _____

9. We would improve our landing craft by doing the following:

    _____

    _____

    _____

    _____

    _____

10. Second Egg Drop Attempt

    When _____

    Where _____

    Results _____

    _____

    _____

    _____

    _____

    _____

Space Creature Writing Web

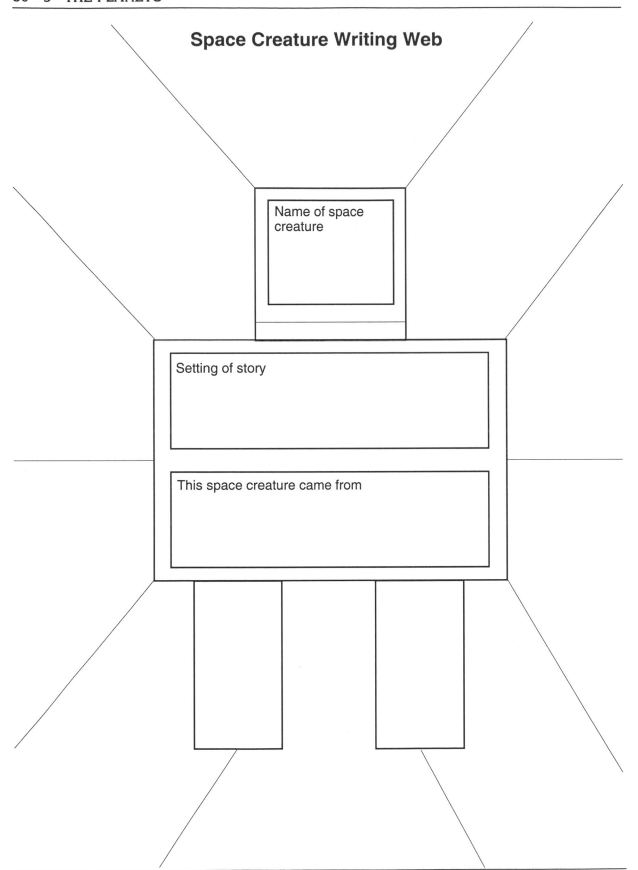

Name of space creature

Setting of story

This space creature came from

Space Creature Writing Web

Instructions

Name _____ Date _____

In addition to the items noted on the creature web, include the following information on any of the lines or spaces on the web. Remember, this story will be similar to *The Indian in the Cupboard*, in which the character has adventures at home and school with his miniature Indian and cowboy. You will be having adventures with the miniature space creature you designed.

- a. Where and how will this creature be stored at home, school, and/or other place, depending on the setting of the story?
- b. What are some of its personality characteristics?
- c. Who are some of the other characters in this story?
- d. What will be the main idea of the story?
- e. How will the story begin?
- f. What are some situations that will take place in the story?
- g. What will the conclusion of the story be?
- h. What are some other items your teacher would like you to include and/or focus upon in this story?

_____

_____

_____

_____

_____

_____

_____

_____

_____

_____

_____

_____

Annotated Bibliography

Banks, Lynne Reid. *The Indian in the Cupboard*. New York: Avon Books, 1980.

Berger, Melvin. *Discovering Mars: The Amazing Story of the Red Planet*. New York: Scholastic, 1992.
An excellent resource and interesting to read for grades 3–5.

"Biodiversity: Earth's Living Treasure." *Odyssey* (October 1992).
Articles and activities regarding Earth's many treasures.

Branley, Franklyn M. *The Sun and the Solar System*. New York: Henry Holt, 1996.
Most of Mr. Branley's books are written for lower elementary students. This book is for upper elementary students, and contains many details about the planets as well as information about a variety of scientific concepts. A good resource for research.

Bruchac, Joseph. *Between Earth and Sky: Legends of Native American Sacred Places*. Orlando, FL: Harcourt Brace, 1996.
Legends and beautiful illustrations dealing with the beauty of and respect for the Earth.

Butterfield, Moira. *1000 Facts About the Earth*. New York: Scholastic, 1992.
A simple, colorful book full of facts.

Cole, Joanna. *The Magic School Bus Inside the Earth*. New York: Scholastic, 1987.

———. *The Magic School Bus Lost in the Solar System*. New York: Scholastic, 1990.

Conrad, Pam. *Call Me Ahnighito*. New York: HarperCollins, 1995.
A delightful picture book that is based on the true story of a meteorite found in 1897 by the Peary Expedition.

d'Aulaire, Ingri, and Edgar Parin d'Aulaire. *d'Aulaires' Book of Greek Myths*. New York: Doubleday, 1962.

Fisher, Leonard, and Everett Fisher. *The Olympians*. New York: Holiday House, 1984.
A picture book containing short synopses of each of the major Greek gods.

"Getting Caught Up in Earth's Atmosphere." *Odyssey* (April 1993).
Articles and activities on the weather in Earth's atmosphere as well as other planets.

Goble, Paul. *Remaking the Earth*. New York: Orchard Books, 1996.
The Great Plains Native Americans' creation story.

Hirst, Robin, and Sally Hirst. *My Place in Space*. New York: Orchard Books, 1988.
A good introductory picture book to a unit of study in astronomy that will appeal to all elementary students.

"Invaders from Space: Asteroids, Meteors, and Comets." *Odyssey* (February 1995).
A whole issue devoted to facts and fiction of asteroids, meteors, and comets. A recipe for making a comet can also be found in this issue.

Kim, Young Jin, comp. *The Blue Planet: A Book of Postcards*. San Francisco: Pomegranate Artbooks, 1995.
Beautiful NASA photographs of Earth taken during Apollo and shuttle missions.

Landau, Elaine. *Saturn*. New York: Franklin Watts, 1991.

Lauber, Patricia. *Seeing Earth from Space*. New York: Scholastic, 1990.
Magnificent NASA photographs of Earth taken during various shuttle missions.

Livingston, Myra Cohn. *Earth Songs*. New York: Scholastic, 1986.
A book of original poems about Earth.

Low, Alice. *The Macmillan Book of Greek Gods and Heroes*. New York: Macmillan, 1985.

Marsh, Carole. *Asteroids, Comets, and Meteors.* New York: Twenty-First Century Books, 1996.
A very detailed and excellent book for use by fourth- and fifth-graders.

Moche, Dinah L. *Astronomy Today.* New York: Random House, 1982.
An excellent reference source for all areas of astronomy that includes superior illustrations.

Mollel, Tololwa. *The Orphan Boy.* New York: Clarion Books, 1990.
A delightful, beautifully illustrated legend of the appearance of Venus in the morning sky and evening sky.

Prelutsky, Jack, comp. *The Random House Book of Poetry for Children.* New York: Random House, 1983.

Ride, Sally, and Tam O'Shaughnessy. *The Third Planet: Exploring the Earth from Space.* New York: Crown, 1994.
Contains NASA photos of Earth with detailed explanations.

Robinson, Fay. *Space Probes to the Planets.* Morton Grove, IL: Albert Whitman, 1993.
Gives details and the findings of NASA's space probes to the planets.

Russell, William F. *Classic Myths to Read Aloud.* New York: Crown, 1989.

Simon, Seymour. *Comets, Meteors, and Asteroids.* New York: Morrow Junior Books, 1994.

———. *Earth: Our Planet in Space.* New York: Macmillan, 1984.

———. *Earth Words: A Dictionary of the Environment.* New York: HarperCollins, 1995.

———. *Jupiter.* New York: Morrow Junior Books, 1985.

———. *Mercury.* New York: Morrow Junior Books, 1992.
Another beautifully illustrated, easy- and quick-to-read, Simon science fact book. Good for grades 1–3.

———. *Neptune.* New York: Morrow Junior Books, 1991.

———. *Saturn.* New York: Morrow Junior Books, 1985.

———. *Uranus.* New York: Morrow Junior Books, 1987.

———. *Venus.* New York: Morrow Junior Books, 1992.

Vogt, Gregory. *Asteroids, Comets, and Meteors.* Brookfield, WI: Millbrook Press, 1996.

———. *Earth.* Brookfield, WI: Millbrook Press, 1996.

———. *Mars.* Brookfield, WI: Millbrook Press, 1994.

———. *Mercury.* Brookfield, WI: Millbrook Press, 1994.
Includes easy-to-read and easy-to-understand facts about the planet Mercury, as well as NASA photos. Dr. Vogt works for NASA's Education Program, and his planet books are appropriate for grades 4–6.

———. *Pluto.* Brookfield, WI: Millbrook Press, 1994.

———. *Venus.* Brookfield, WI: Millbrook Press, 1994.
A glossary is included with each of Dr. Vogt's planet books, along with a section called "Quick Facts."

References and Resources

Asimov, Isaac. *A Distant Puzzle: The Planet Uranus.* Milwaukee, WI: Gareth Stevens, 1994.

Blue Planet. Washington, DC: Office of Education, National Air and Space Museum, 1990.
Contains information and activities related to Earth science.

Caduto, Michael J., and Joseph Bruchac. *Keepers of the Night: Native American Stories and Nocturnal Activities for Children.* Golden, CO: Fulcrum, 1994.

Along with the legends, contains a variety of comprehension, writing, and hands-on activities.

Daily, Robert. *Earth*. New York: Franklin Watts, 1994.

Earth's Mysterious Atmosphere: Atlas 1 Teacher's Guide with Activities. Washington, DC: NASA, 1992.

Explore New Worlds Through Science and Technology. Arlington, VA: National Science Foundation, 1995.

Freeman, Sara E. *Our Solar System: Ideas and Activities Across the Curriculum*. Palos Verdes Estates, CA: Frank Schaffer Publications, 1992.

Mandell, Muriel. *Simple Weather Experiments with Everyday Materials*. New York: Sterling, 1990.
The experiments on water, weather, and air are easy to do and provide oohs and aahs from elementary students when understanding is realized.

Our Mission to Planet Earth: A Guide to Teaching Earth System Science. Washington, DC: NASA Office of Education, 1994.

"Outer Limits." *Philadelphia Inquirer* Supplement. June 2, 1992.

Schatz, Dennis, and Doug Cooper. *Astro Adventures*. Seattle, WA: Pacific Science Center, 1994.

Spence, Lewis. *North American Indians: Myths and Legends*. Studio Editions Ltd. London: Princess House, 1994.

Teaching with Themes: Environments. New York: Scholastic, 1993.
Includes teaching tips and three picture books about Earth.

Using Nonfiction Effectively in Your Classroom. Danbury, CT: Grolier, 1995.
A good teacher resource when looking for change-of-pace ideas for the classroom.

VanCleave, Janice. *Weather*. New York: John Wiley, 1995.

Winrich, Ralph A. *Nergal, the 4th Planet: An Exercise in Imagination*. Cleveland, OH: NASA Lewis Research Center, 1988.
Elementary activities for studying Mars.

Young Astronaut Program. *At Home in the Universe*. Vol. 6. Washington, DC: Young Astronaut Council, 1997.

———. *Biosphere 2*. Vol. 6. Washington, DC: Young Astronaut Council, January/February 1991.
Provides activities on all biomes.

———. *Earth: A View from Space*. Vol. 10. Washington, DC: Young Astronaut Council, 1995.
Activities regarding water and effects of erosion.

———. *Earth Search, Part II*. Washington, DC: Young Astronaut Council, 1997.
Contributes activities on land, water, air, and life on Earth.

———. *Galileo to Jupiter*. Vol. 5. Washington, DC: Young Astronaut Council, November 1989.
Activities revolving around the spacecraft Galileo and its journey to and investigation of Jupiter.

———. *Mission to Mars*. Vol. 4. Washington, DC: Young Astronaut Council, December 1988.
Elementary, hands-on activities regarding planet Mars.

———. *Our Fragile Future*. Vol. 8. Washington, DC: Young Astronaut Council, February/March 1993.
Furnishes activities on water recycling, clouds, weather, and global warming.

———. *Return to Mars*. Vol. 8. Washington, DC: Young Astronaut Council, December/January 1992–93.
Several different elementary-level activities dealing with the landform features of Mars.

——. *Voyager: The Grand Tour.* Washington, DC: Young Astronaut Council, October/November 1990.

Musical Resources

Holst, Gustav. *The Planets, Op.32.* Andre Previn and the Royal Philharmonic Orchestra. Cleveland, OH: TELARC, 1986.

Electronic Sources

Allen, Jesse S. 1997. *Webstars: Astronomy Resources on the World Wide Web.* URL: http://heasarc.gsfc.nasa.gov/docs/www_info/webstars.html (Accessed July 19, 1997).
Many, many excellent links.

Arnett, Bill. 1997. *The Nine Planets.* 1994–95. URL: http://www.deepspace.ucsb.edu/ia/nineplanets/nineplanets.html (Accessed July 9, 1997).
Look for the special sections on comets and asteroids in addition to the detailed information about planets.

Benson, Jeff, and Florence Vaughn. 1997. *The Martian Sun-Times.* URL: http://www.ucls.uchicago.edu/MartianSunTimes (Accessed July 19, 1997).
Gives information about the weather on Earth and Mars.

Brewster, Stephen C. 1997. *Ice and Fire: Pluto-Kuiper Express.* URL: http://www.jpl.nasa.gov/pluto (Accessed July 15, 1997).
A future space probe mission to Pluto.

California Institute of Technology. 1997. *Welcome to the Planets.* URL: http://pds.jpl.nasa.gov/planets (Accessed July 9, 1997).

Cassini Homepage. 1997. URL: http://www.jpl.nasa.gov/cassini (Accessed July 14, 1997).
This is the homepage for the Saturn space probe due to arrive on Saturn in 2004.

Cummins, R. Hays. 1997. *Sources for Earth Science and Astronomy.* URL: http://jrscience.wcp.muohio.edu/html/earthsci.html (Accessed July 15, 1997).

Dubov, David. 1997. *The Martian Chronicle Home Page.* URL: http://www.jpl.nasa.gov/mars/MartianChronicle (Accessed July 19, 1997).

Feldman, Gene Carl. 1997. *Ocean Planet Homepage.* URL: http://seawifs.gsfc.nasa.gov/ocean_planet.html (Accessed July 15, 1997).
This is an online exhibit developed by NASA and the Natural History Museum at the Smithsonian Institute.

Galileo Homepage. 1997. URL: http://www.jpl.nasa.gov/galileo (Accessed July 14, 1997).
This is the homepage for the Galileo spacecraft, which has investigated Jupiter and its four Galilean moons.

Goodall, Kirk. 1997. *Mars Pathfinder Mission.* URL: http://mpfwww.arc.nasa.gov (Accessed July 13, 1997).

Hamilton, Calvin J. 1997. *Views of the Solar System.* 1996–97. URL: http://bang.lanl.gov/solarsys/ (Accessed July 13, 1997).
In addition to planets, look for the section on asteroids.

Kronk, Gary. 1997. *Gary Kronk's Comet Page.* 1995. URL: http://medicine.wustl.edu/~kronkg/comet.html (Accessed July 20, 1997).

Maris Multimedia. 1997. *Solar System Explorer.* URL: http://www.maris.com/ssehome.htm (Accessed July 19, 1997).

Mars Global Surveyor. 1997. URL: http://mgs-www.jpl.nasa.gov (Accessed July 13, 1997).

Mars Pathfinder Home Page. 1997. URL: http://mpfwww.jpl.nasa.gov/default.html (Accessed July 5, 1997).

NASA K–12 Internet Initiative. 1997. URL: http://quest.arc.nasa.gov (Accessed July 19, 1997).

This is an excellent site with links to all kinds of planetary and other space-related projects. Look for "Live From Mars," "Shuttle Team Online," and "Women of NASA."

Reston Communications. 1997. *The Whole Mars Catalog.* URL: http://www.reston.com/astro/mars/catalog.html (Accessed July 19, 1997).

Sky Publishing Corporation. 1997. *Sky Online's Comet Page.* URL: http://www.skypub.com/comets/comets.html (Accessed July 20, 1997).

University of Michigan Regents. 1997. *Windows to the Universe.* 1995–97. URL: http://www.windows.umich.edu (Accessed July 13, 1997).

One of the best websites I have seen. Enter the website and click into any area: "Poetry," "Space Mission Headlines," "Our Solar System," "Our Planet," "Myths." Be sure to preview the myths area: Some versions of the myths, as well as the corresponding art, contain sexual content that may be inappropriate for elementary-age students.

Williams, Dr. David. 1997. *Planetary Sciences at NSSDC* (National Space Science Data Center). URL: http://nssdc.gsfc.nasa.gov/planetary/planetary_home.html (Accessed July 19, 1997).

Click into information on all planets plus asteroids and comets.

Yocum, Karen. *Mission to Planet Earth.* 1997. URL: http://www.hq.nasa.gov/office/mpte/education.html (Accessed July 19, 1997).

CHAPTER 4

Star Bright, Star Light

Introducing stars to students is my favorite part of studying the night sky, because of all the wonderful tales and legends from various cultures that go along with the patterns of the stars. Students are fascinated by the marvelous stories and are anxious to search for the **pictures** in the sky. In this chapter you will find a wide range of books and stories from which to choose, along with language, art, math, and science activities as accompaniments to these tales. Use them to develop interest in learning about the stars, as well as in acquiring knowledge of the stars and constellations.

Developing Interest

On a piece of paper, have students brainstorm what they think when they look at stars, what they think they know about stars, and what they would like to know about stars. After discussing the brainstorming, have students keep this sheet and all the information from this unit in pocket folders to be used as their star folders. Complete the sheet again at the end of the unit and compare. Students should create an illustration on the cover of the folders based on some of their brainstorming ideas.

Introductory Story Choices

Choose any of the following stories to read aloud as an introductory story for your students, referring to the bibliography for information about each book. Choose from "The Scattered Stars" found in *The Earth Under Sky Bear's Feet*, *Children of the Stars*, or *The Sky Is Full of Stars*, and complete the sequencing activity described below as a follow-up.

➤ Before reading the story aloud, prepare a large star cutout on which a small portion of the story has been written for each student or pair of students.

➤ After reading the story, give each student or pair one of the stars, and have each create an illustration to go with that section of the story.

➤ Students should then read each other's stars, stand in front of the room with their stars and drawings so that they are arranged in the sequence of the story, and re-tell the story.

➤ Display the stars and the drawings around the room as a reminder of this first tale.

If you wish to use all of the story suggestions, have small groups choose different stories and complete the same sequencing activity for each of the tales, giving everyone the chance to hear all of the accounts as to how stars got into the sky.

Follow-Up Legends and Activities

The following three legends recount in greater detail how the stars came to be in the night sky: *How the Stars Fell Into the Sky*, *The Story of the Milky Way*, and *Min-Yo and the Moon Dragon*. The following language arts activity, creating a recipe booklet, is one you may wish to try with your students.

➤ You will need two of each of the books listed above so that you can divide the class into six groups.

➤ Rotate the books among the groups so that each will read all three stories.

➤ All students should have three copies each of the reproducibles "Star Recipes: Organizing Thoughts During Reading" and "Recipe for the Stars" (see pages 107 and 108–9).

➤ Have students complete the reproducibles as they read each story. (See pages 89 and 90 for two recipe examples.)

➤ When students complete the reading and writing for all three stories, have them write an editorial that states which of the star stories best explains how the stars came to be. (Be sure students support their opinions.)

➤ Create a cover, and combine the star recipes and editorial to create a star recipe booklet.

➤ *Student Example*

How the Stars Fell Into the Sky

Jerrie Oughton

Name of Student: Date: January 24, 1997

Ingredients:

    100,000 jewels

    one coyote

    sky

    one woman

Directions:

First, have woman write in the sky with jewels.

Then, let coyote help woman.

Third, make the coyote get impatient.

Fourth, let coyote throw jewels into the sky.

When you are finished, you will have a pretty sky, full of light.

Andy Clark, Fourth Grade,
Tatem School, Haddonfield, NJ

➤ *Student Example*

Min-Yo and the Moon Dragon

Elizabeth Hillman

Name of Student: Date: January 27, 1997

Ingredients:

    Diamonds from the cave on the Moon

    Moon Dragon

    Light Child

    Moon

    Cobweb staircase

Directions:

First, let the Moon fall and let Light Child climb the cobweb staircase to find out why Moon is falling.

Then, let Light Child give Moon Dragon a diamond as a gift and bribery.

Third, ask Moon Dragon to stop Moon from hitting Earth.

Fourth, throw the diamonds into the sky to have less weight on the Moon.

Fifth, let Light Child go back to Earth.

When you are finished you will have stars in the sky made by Light Child and Moon Dragon.

Mackenzie Lovell, Fourth Grade,
Tatem School, Haddonfield, NJ

Discovering the Constellations

Based on literature, students now know how the stars got into the sky; therefore it is time to find the patterns of the stars and their related star stories. In the Western world, constellation names come from Greek mythology, as do many of the stories about them; however, there are tales from other cultures that illustrate the stories of the star patterns. Because students will need to do some night viewing of the sky, you may want to send a note home to parents letting them know you will be requesting that students observe various constellations on clear nights, and parents may need to assist students by accompanying them and finding a safe observation place free of light pollution. Suggest to students that a piece of red cellophane placed over a flashlight will allow them to read their star finders while they are outside observing the night sky.

I find that the Fall/Winter sky is easier to observe, because it gets dark early and there are no leaves on the trees. The constellations that appear at this time of year seem to have more stories that are of interest to the students, as well, although the Spring/Summer sky should not be ignored.

Introduction to the Constellations

Begin by using the original play *Callisto and Zeus*, the story of the Big and Little Dippers (see pages 92–93). As a language activity, do the following:

1. Read through the play with students and divide the class into groups of five.

2. Each group should plan and present their interpretation of the play using small homemade props and costumes. You will find that although everyone is reenacting the same play, students will be very imaginative, finding different ways to perform and interpret the play.

3. Once students are familiar with the myth of the Big and Little Dippers, follow up with the science activity after the play (see page 94).

Callisto and Zeus

An original play by Joanne Letwinch

The Story of the Great Bear and Little Bear
and How the Dippers Came to Be

Characters: Zeus
              Callisto
              Hera
              Arcus
              Narrator

Zeus: I am Zeus, King of the Gods. I live on Mt. Olympus, but I have come to visit Earth.

Callisto: I am Callisto, a beautiful forest nymph.

Zeus: I love you Callisto. Will you marry me?

Callisto: I know I should not marry you, but I love you, and I will.

Narrator: Meanwhile, back at Mt. Olympus, the home of the Gods, we meet Hera.

Hera: I am Hera, Zeus's wife and the queen of marriage. I am furious that my husband has married such a beautiful Earth maiden. I hear that Callisto has given birth to a son. I am so full of rage that I shall visit Earth and punish Callisto.

Narrator: Callisto sees Hera as Hera arrives on Earth.

Callisto: Oh, Hera, I beg of you, please forgive me. I know I was wrong. Please do not harm me or my son, Arcus.

Hera: I am outraged. You shall be punished and will never be beautiful again. We shall see how Zeus likes that!

Narrator: Hera decided to turn Callisto into a great bear. Callisto became covered with coarse, black hair, and developed large paws, giant teeth, and a fierce growl. Arcus was unharmed, but screamed in fear as Callisto approached him. The other forest nymphs took Arcus away to live with another family.

Callisto: I know everyone is afraid of me now, and the hunters are after me, but I will try to stay as close to my son as possible.

Arcus:	It seems to me that whenever I am sleeping or walking in the forest, I feel as though a great bear is watching me.
Narrator:	Time passes.
Callisto:	The hunters keep coming after me, and I am being forced further and further into the deep woods. I am far from my son, and I dream about him always. When spring comes, I will return to the part of the forest in which Arcus lives.
Narrator:	Spring arrives and Callisto returns.
Callisto:	There is a hunter shooting at a lovely bird. Could it be Arcus?
Narrator:	Callisto's movements attract the hunter.
Arcus:	A great bear! Is that the one whom I feared was once watching me? I shall shoot it with my bow and arrow.
Narrator:	Callisto just stood there in horror and could not understand why her son wished to shoot her.
Zeus:	As I watch over Earth, I see that my son Arcus is about to kill the beautiful young forest nymph that I once loved. I must act quickly to save her.
Narrator:	As fast as a lightning bolt, Zeus grabbed Callisto's tail and threw her into the night sky near the North Pole. He changed Arcus into a small bear and threw him into the sky to live beside his mother. As they lived in the night sky, they both became beautiful stars.
Hera:	I am shocked that the great bear and the small bear have become beautiful stars in the heavens. I will call on Poseidon, god of the sea. Poseidon, be sure that the stars of the great bear and the little bear never plunge into the ocean so that they may wash, as other stars do.
Narrator:	The Great Bear (Ursa Major) and the Little Bear (Ursa Minor) continue to live happily ever after together in the night sky. Because they do not dip below the horizon *to wash*, they do not shine quite as brightly as other stars. These stars are better known as the Big Dipper and the Little Dipper.

Constructing and Using a Star Finder

1. Use the star finder pattern and instructions found in *Astro Adventures* to allow each student to make and operate a star finder. There are commercially made star finders; however, I have found this to be one of the best. Students enjoy making it, and it is easy for them to use.

2. Play inspirational star music while making the star finders; you will find some suggestions in the bibliography.

3. On the star finder, locate the Big and Little Dippers, and have students note the shapes of the two dippers. Use manipulatives so that students may feel and visualize the shape, allowing students to more easily find the patterns in the night sky.

4. Check with your Kindergarten or first-grade colleagues because they generally have a pretty good supply of cubes, pattern blocks, puzzle pieces, etc., that can be used as manipulatives. Colored toothpicks and bingo chips are also useful when practicing the constellation patterns.

5. I usually start with centimeter cubes and distribute them in small plastic bags to students. Students should use the cubes to re-create the shapes of the Big and Little Dippers on their desktops, being sure to position the two dippers correctly so that the North Star is properly placed. The North Star is the last star in the tail of the Little Dipper, and is found by following the pointer stars in the bowl of the Big Dipper.

6. Be sure to let students know that the Big and Little Dippers are part of the larger constellations Ursa Major and Ursa Minor.

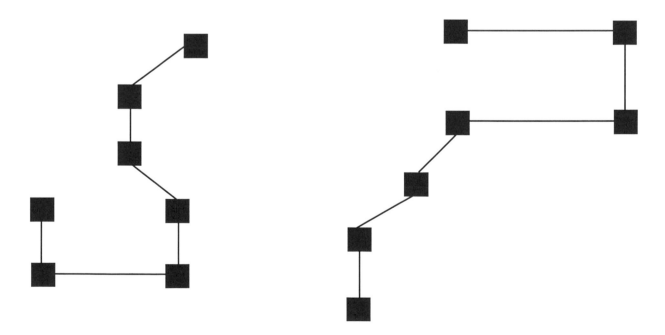

Placement of centimeter cubes in the positions of the Big and Little Dippers as seen on January 1 at 8 P.M.

➤ *Art Activity: Big and Little Dippers*

Each student will need a 9-by-12-inch piece of black construction paper, and fourteen small, stick-on white dots (found in stationery stores).

1. Students should observe their cube structures, and using the white dots, reproduce the Big and Little Dippers on the black paper.

2. Students should take these home, along with their star finders, and observe the two dippers in the night sky.

➤ *Keeping a Journal*

As students travel through the night sky, have them document their adventures in the form of a travel guide. Before writing, students should look through travel guides and brochures to get an idea as to how these items are written. Record on a class chart common items and forms of writing, especially vocabulary, found in travel brochures. Have students refer to this chart as they write their own travel guide to the stars.

Write the first journal entry as a class, using students' travels to the Big and Little Dippers. Brainstorm and emphasize the use of descriptive vocabulary as well as specific characterizations of each constellation. Have students use the reproducible "Travel Journal" to complete their own adventures (page 110).

Example:

Are you thinking of visiting the fabulous constellations of Ursa Major and Minor? Do it today! These superb destinations are good starting points for your travels through the winter sky. You will find the polished seven stars of the Big Dipper inviting and heavenly, as the two stars of its bowl guide you to the North Star. While Ursa Minor may not be as bright, you will find this Little Bear very friendly and eager to direct you to other marvelous constellations in the night sky, especially those nearby. Check tonight with your local astronomer or star map to find the best viewing and visiting times for the Big and Little Dippers. Hope you'll visit us soon.

Continuing Travels Through the Constellations

➤ *Cassiopeia: Literature and Science*

The second stop on the students' trip through the constellations is Cassiopeia, the Evil Queen. Her story can be found in *The Macmillan Book of Greek Gods and Heroes*, *Star Tales:*

North American Indian Stories About the Stars, and *Glow-in-the-Dark Constellations*. After reading Cassiopeia's story, complete the following science/literature/art activity.

➤   Have students find Cassiopeia on their star finders and reconstruct her pattern using the centimeter cubes, or other manipulatives, as described in the activity on page 94.

➤   Retell Cassiopeia's story using a story web in the shape of her constellation.

Have students make five large yellow construction-paper stars and summarize the story of Cassiopeia in five parts.

Write one main event on each of the first four stars, and on the fifth star, write the ending of the story along with an explanation for Cassiopeia's shape and placement in the night sky.

Glue all five stars onto 12-by-18-inch black construction paper in the shape of Cassiopeia, being sure that the stars are in sequence, retelling Cassiopeia's story accurately.

Display the finished products and have students find Cassiopeia in the night sky.

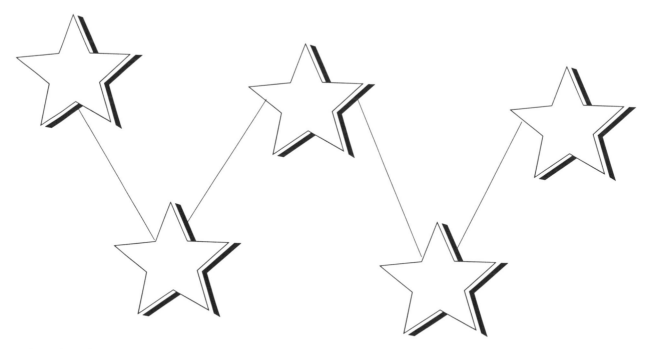

Cassiopeia.

Example of what might be written on each of the five stars.

Star one: The queen of Ethiopia, Cassiopeia, boasted about her beauty.

Star two: The sea nymphs were angry. Poseidon, the god of the sea, sent a sea monster to destroy Ethiopia.

Star three: To save Ethiopia, Cassiopeia's daughter, Andromeda, was offered to Cetus, the sea monster, as a sacrifice.

Star four: Perseus saved Andromeda from Cetus.

Star five: When Cassiopeia died, she was punished by being placed in an uncomfortable position in the sky.

Students should add to their travel journals detailing a visit to Cassiopeia.

➤ *Cassiopeia's Family: Literature*

Now that students know Cassiopeia's story, they should read about her immediate family and visit them as the third stop on the trip through the constellations—Cepheus, her husband; Andromeda, her daughter; Perseus, her son-in-law; and Cetus, the monster whale that destroys Ethiopia. Point out to students, as they look at their star finders, that all these constellations are located near one another in the night sky. Stories of Cassiopeia's family can be found in the following: Perseus, *The Macmillan Book of Greek Gods and Heroes* and *Perseus and Medusa*; Perseus and Andromeda, *The Book of Dragons*; Cetus, *The Heavenly Zoo*; Cepheus, *The Stargazer Guide to the Galaxy*. Complete the following language arts activity after reading the stories of each of these mythological characters.

➢ Use the reproducible "Cassiopeia's Family" (see page 111), and the "Limerick" suggestions found in Chapter 6 (see pages 152–53).

➢ Have students refer to the character traits as they write a limerick about each of the constellation characters in Cassiopeia's family, and place each limerick on a 4-by-6-inch index card for use in the science/art activities that follow.

➤ *Cassiopeia's Family: Science/Art*

Because there are several constellations involved, have students work in groups of four.

Using the date on which you are doing this activity, and the time of eight or nine o'clock. Have students locate each member of Cassiopeia's family on their star finders and note their shapes. To complete the following activity, each group of four students will need: a set of pattern blocks, a 36-by-48-inch piece of black butcher paper, blue pipe cleaners, white stick-on stars or labeling dots, and a jar of rubber cement.

1. Make sure each group of students has a large floor or table area in which to work. Using pattern blocks, practice reconstructing the shape of each constellation on top of the black butcher paper. It usually works best if each student has an assigned constellation in Cassiopeia's family, with all group members helping one another to form all the patterns correctly. Check to be certain that students place the blocks properly so that they are re-creating the shapes and the positions as they are shown on the star finder.

2. Request that students now use their pipe cleaners to create the shape of their assigned constellation, remove the pattern blocks, and glue the pipe cleaner shape in place of the blocks.

3. Students should then properly position the white dots on top of the pipe cleaners so that the dots represent each of the stars in the constellation. Remind students to be patient with the rubber cement, because it sometimes takes awhile for the pipe cleaners to adhere properly to the paper.

4. Staple the limerick index cards created in the language activity along the bottom of the black paper. Write a title such as "Cassiopeia's Family of Stars" at the top, and display.

Again have students journal a visit to Cassiopeia's family.

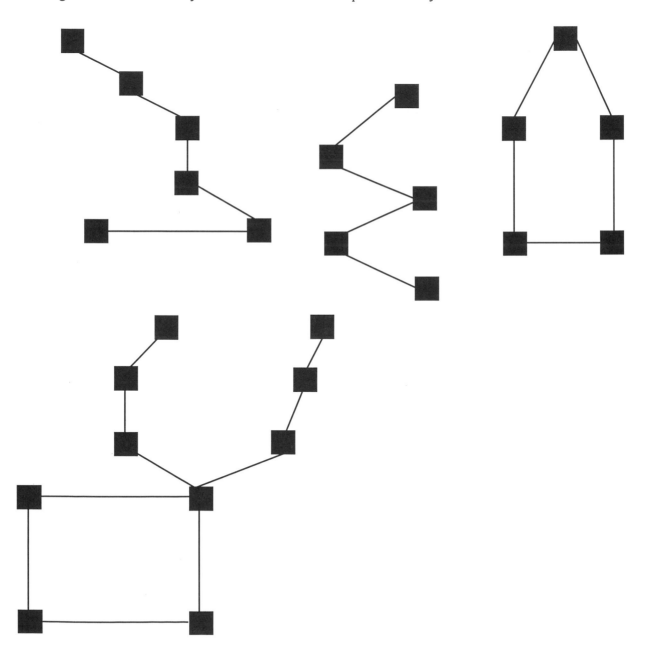

Cassiopeia's Family, April 1, 8 P.M.

➤ *Constellation Choices and Literature Responses*

Now that students are familiar with finding some of the constellations, reading their corresponding stories, and responding to literature in a variety of ways, have students choose the next stop on their journey through the night sky. Following are some constellation stories that students particularly enjoy reading.

> ➤ Orion: "The Race for the Prize Fish" from *Star Tales*; *The Macmillan Book of Greek Gods and Heroes*; *Constellations* (myths from various cultures).

> ➤ Draco: *The Heavenly Zoo*; "Golden Apples" from *The Way of the Stars*. These two stories tell the story of Draco in completely different ways, but students enjoy both of them.

> ➤ Hercules/Heracles: *The Macmillan Book of Greek Gods and Heroes*.

> ➤ The Pleiades or Seven Sisters (found in the constellation of Taurus, the Bull, during the winter): "The Dancing Braves" from *Star Tales*, and "The Boastful Star" found in *Tales of the Shimmering Sky*.

> ➤ Canis Major: *The Heavenly Zoo*.

> ➤ Swan (a very easy constellation to spot in the summer sky): *The Heavenly Zoo,* or "The Spirit of the Snow Goose" from *Star Tales*.

Story summaries of all these constellations can also be found in *The Stargazers*. Have students complete this following activity: Students should read the story about the constellation they have chosen, and find it on the star finder. Direct students to create bright, colorful, and descriptive posters, approximately 12 by 18 inches, advertising the constellation about which they have read. The poster should include a picture of the constellation, its name, information as to how it became a constellation, and why it should be visited.

➤ *End of the Journey*

To complete their travels through the constellations, direct students to read the story that corresponds with their zodiac sign and complete the suggested activity. Zodiac constellation stories can be found in *The Shining Stars*, *Stories from the Stars*, or *The Heavenly Zoo*.

1. Assist students in determining their zodiac signs, locating its corresponding constellation on the star finder, and reading its story. Tell students to look along the ecliptic on their star finders to find all the zodiac constellations.

2. Students should then re-create their zodiac constellation, first mapping it with a manipulative activity, and then drawing it on 12-by-18-inch black construction paper using glow-in-the-dark paint.

3. Have students use a contrasting color of 18-by-24-inch construction paper as a frame for the picture, and then glue or staple the black paper onto the frame paper.

4. On a 5-by-8-inch index card, write a caption for the picture which summarizes the story of this zodiac constellation. Pair students with someone who has a different zodiac sign and have the partners share their pictures and stories.

5. To hold students accountable for listening to their partner's zodiac story, have them create a birthday card for their partner including their partner's birthdate, the name of the zodiac sign, and a poem, such as a series of couplets or a cinquain, giving some information about their partner's zodiac constellation story.

6. Instead of or in addition to the poems, you may wish to direct students to write a paragraph or two describing similarities and/or differences between their zodiac story and their partner's.

7. Allow students to take home their zodiac constellation picture to keep in their bedrooms, requesting that they get permission from their parents before placing it on the ceiling.

Students should end their travel journals by describing a vacation trip to their own zodiac constellation. Have students put all their travel journals into booklet form, perhaps adding a picture postcard (use index cards) to the last page illustrating a particularly memorable visit.

Constellation Stories and Websites

Chris Dolan's Constellation Page at http://www.astro.wisc.edu/~dolan/constellations/ (as of March, 1997) provides summaries of most of the constellation stories. This is especially helpful because there are stories of some of the constellations that are often hard to find. The website also provides links to sky charts. Printing the sky charts for the familiar constellations and allowing them to trace over the pattern gives students a chance to see the constellation patterns surrounded by other stars (as they really will be in the night sky).

Another website (as of March, 1997) that furnishes sky charts is: http://www.physics. csbsju.edu/astro. Click into "Constellations to Know." This site offers positive, dark sky charts for a variety of constellations, and each constellation comes as a set. One graphic depicts the constellations with a dark sky background, white stars, and the outline of the constellation, and the other is the same graphic without the pattern line. Try the following activity after students have become *very* familiar with some of the constellation patterns and have used manipulatives to create the constellation patterns.

➢   Print copies of both types of charts, put them on transparencies, and give students copies of the constellation without the pattern lines.

➢   First display the transparency with the pattern lines for a minute or so, remove it, and then reveal the transparency without the pattern lines.

➢   Have students outline the constellation on their papers, allowing students to visualize the night sky as it really is.

Investigate, also, *Mike Boschat's Astronomy Page* at http://www.atm.dal.ca/~andromed (as of July 7, 1997). This page literally covers all astronomy topics from A to Z with numerous links. *NASA Observatorium* at http://observe.ivv.nasa.gov/nasa/core.shtml (as of July 7, 1997) contains an image gallery and a separate link for stars.

Writing a Constellation Myth

1.   Now that students have traveled to distant stars, tell them that they are going to have the opportunity to design their own constellation.

2.   Ask them to think about the constellation characters they have already met and the myths they have read, and review and list these with students.

3.   Based on that information, ask students what object(s) or person they might choose if they were to design a constellation myth.

4.   Brainstorm ideas and encourage students to think about something that may have special meaning for them. Remind them that although constellations sometimes became part of the night sky as punishment, most of the time it was an honor. I have had a student who paid tribute to her recently deceased grandfather, while other students have chosen sports or entertainment figures or special pets.

5.   Once each student has decided on an object/person, each should create a constellation by mapping it with centimeter cubes or other manipulative object. When students are satisfied with their creations, they should draw them on paper.

6. From that point, students should plan their constellation myth by incorporating all the facets of good story-writing (character descriptions, setting, sequence of events, etc.) and follow the writing process. As part of their myth, students may wish to include some of the constellation characters and places they have already encountered.

7. Using a copy of a star chart for the current month (*Science and Children* from NSTA [National Science Teachers Association] and *Astronomy* carry them), have students find locations for their constellations.

8. Students may wish to display their original constellation simply by sketching on black paper with white crayons or paint. If you would like to conclude the writing task with a whole-class or small-group project, try creating a mini-planetarium or star chart using the new constellations.

   * Use a large piece (at least 36 by 24 inches) of black posterboard or butcher paper, and cut the paper into a circular shape.

   * Using white paint, place Ursa Major and Minor as they would appear at the time of year you are doing this activity.

   * Students should then paint and label their newly created constellations around the circumpolar constellations.

   * Exhibit this original star chart along with the students' myths.

More Star Events

Literature, Science, Art

The ideas suggested here can be used with any or all of the constellation myths. The first is a version of the "Box Planetarium" taken from *Astronomy for Every Kid* by Janice VanCleave. Follow the first three steps in the original experiment. For the fourth step, instead of putting pinholes anywhere on the black paper, have students poke the holes so that they create a specific constellation pattern. Proceed by following the remainder of the directions. Each student or small group can create their own planetarium box depicting a different constellation.

The next idea is courtesy of Ellie, my fifth-grade colleague. She told me not to mention her name, but this is her idea, so she gets the credit. Create a planetarium of constellations that hang from the classroom ceiling by using tongue depressors, glue, and circles approximately one inch in diameter, cut from posterboard and painted with glow-in-the-dark paint. Create each constellation by attaching the circles, representing the stars, to the tongue depressors in the proper positions for that constellation and write the name of the constellation along one of the tongue depressors. Hang each constellation from the ceiling in an arrangement that would follow, as closely as possible, the night sky on a particular night and time, and instruct students to write a summary of the story that corresponds with the constellation they constructed. As an alternative, paint small Styrofoam balls with glow-in-the-dark paint, using them as star representations, then connect them with craft sticks or toothpicks to form the constellations.

Star Poetry

Throughout the ages, people have wondered, written, and romanticized about stars. There are a number of poems written about stars, many of which appeal to children. Two books to use are Seymour Simon's *Starwalk* and Myra Cohn Livingston's *Space Songs*. *Starwalk* is a collection of space and star poetry written by others, and *Space Songs*, a book of original poems, ranges over a variety of space topics. Other poems that can be found in a variety of children's poetry books are highlighted here.

My favorite poem is "When I Heard the Learn'd Astronomer" written by Walt Whitman, found in *Starwalk*, as well as several other poetry anthologies. I think it says everything there is to say about astronomy and skywatching. One can do all the math and science associated with astronomy, but when it's all over, there is nothing better than simply observing and appreciating what is there.

Other star poems that students enjoy are "Summer Stars" by Carl Sandburg, "Somebody Has To" from *A Light in the Attic* by Shel Silverstein, "A Shooting Star" by Edith M. Thomas, "The Falling Star" by Sara Teasdale, and "My Star" by Marion Kennedy. Two versions of "Twinkle, Twinkle Little Star" are enjoyable to students, one by Jane Taylor, and the other in paperback and picture form by Iza Tapani. You may wish to read aloud the latter as inspiration prior to students journeying to the constellations. Have students complete several activities based on some of these poems, referring to the section on poetry in Chapter 6 for ideas.

➤ *Writing Poetry*

Once students have completed a number of poetry tasks, encourage them to write some of their own. I like to start with the poem "At Nighttime" by Aileen Fisher. Give each student a copy of the poem. Read it aloud as they listen or choral read it. Assign the parts of the snow, maple trees, and stars to be performed as the poem is read. Have each student brainstorm a list of nighttime wondering thoughts they may have. As they finish that assignment, have students use their brainstorming ideas to write their own nighttime wondering poem, keeping the first verse as is. Students then write their own variations of the next three verses using only the first two words of verses two and four, and the first three words of the third verse. Illustrations of their poems should complete students' own versions of nighttime wondering thoughts.

Add music to your poetry as well. In *Our Solar System*, a teacher resource book from Frank Schaffer, you will find the song "We're a Travelin' Through Our Solar System," sung to the tune of "She'll Be Comin' Round the Mountain." Have students change this a bit, to "We're a Travelin' to the Constellations Now!" Instead of each verse concerning one of the planets, rewrite the verses to fit the constellations to which students have traveled. Sing a verse or two each day, or make it more elaborate by creating a whole musical production.

➤ *Star Vocabulary*

Following is a list of vocabulary words that can be used throughout the unit. A regular children's dictionary is a good source of definitions, as well as *The Young Astronomer*. For additional background for the teacher, consult the *Dictionary of Astronomy*.

Asteroid	Light Year
Astrolabe	Magnitude
Astronomical Unit	Meteor
Astronomy	Meteorite
Atmosphere	Meteoroid
Binary Star	Milky Way
Black Hole	Nebula
Celestial	Nova
Celestial Equator	Observatory
Comet	Red Giant
Constellation	Star
Dwarf Star	Stellar
Ecliptic	Sun
Galaxy	Supergiant
Light Pollution	Supernova

➤ *Star Rings*

1. Create a star template for each student using the star pattern on the next page. The template should fit a 9-by-12-inch piece of construction paper.

2. Students should use the template to produce ten to twelve stars, and a hole should be punched at the top of each star.

3. Use large notebook rings to hold the stars together.

4. As vocabulary is introduced, students should write the words and their definitions on the stars, being sure to use both sides and adding paper stars to the rings, as needed.

5. Encourage students to add astronomy-based vocabulary words in which they are interested or may discover on their own, and advocate the use of the vocabulary in students' journals or other writing assignments.

6. To store the vocabulary rings and create a bulletin board at the same time, place drapery hooks around the edge of a bulletin board and have students place their rings on the drapery hooks.

7. Assign a small set of words to pairs of students to illustrate, label, and post on the bulletin board, or guide students in designing a picture dictionary using the vocabulary words.

➤ A Star Party

Probably one of the most enjoyable ways to end a unit about stars is to have a star party, and it can be done in an organized, but informal, way. Of course, this will need to be done at night, so it is probably best to do it in late fall or early spring, before Daylight Savings Time begins. Select a date, including a rain date and/or a cloudy night date, a time, a place, and invite students and parents. For crowd control, it is best to allow only the students in your class and their parents, and enlist the help of room parents in organizing and perhaps providing refreshments. Request that students bring their star finders and flashlights with red filters and certainly binoculars and telescopes if they have them. Send home patterns and materials for star finders ahead of time, so that the adults can make them and have them available for their use as well, or you may ask a room parent or two to hold a session for making star finders prior to the big night. Be sure to review with students, ahead of time, the night sky for that date, and investigate the possibility of inviting a trained astronomer or someone from a local amateur astronomy club. The party does not have to last more than an hour, but it is exciting to watch students apply their classroom knowledge.

Give students the opportunity to learn about a new constellation that evening. Select one that will be in the sky during the night of the party, but one with which the students may not be familiar. Read the story aloud that night, find it on the star finder, and then find it in the night sky. Have a star-studded evening!

This chapter, as with all the chapters, has just touched the tip of the iceberg regarding a study of the stars. My hope is that it has encouraged and inspired you and your students to read, study, and learn a little bit about the night sky, and that all of you will take some time to continue learning and observing on your own. Happy Stargazing!

Star Recipes: Organizing Thoughts During Reading

Name _____ Date _____

Directions:

1. As you read one of the stories about how stars came to be, complete this page.

2. On the "Recipe for the Stars" page, do the following:
    a. Use the information from this worksheet to help you write the recipe.
    b. Use the box to illustrate your recipe.

Title of book/story _____

Main Characters   _____

                         _____

                         _____

                         _____

Main Events

1. _____

2. _____

3. _____

4. _____

5. _____

The stars got into the sky in this story because

_____

_____

_____

_____

Recipe for the Stars

Title of book _____

Author _____

Name _____ Date _____

Ingredients:

_____

_____

_____

_____

_____

Directions:

First,

_____

_____

Then,

_____

_____

Third,

_____

_____

Fourth,

_____

_____

When you are finished you will have a

_____

_____

_____

_____

Travel Journal

Name _____   Date _____

Constellation visited

_____

_____

_____

_____

_____

_____

_____

_____

_____

_____

_____

_____

_____

_____

_____

_____

_____

Cassiopeia's Family

Character Traits

Name _____ Date _____

Directions: After reading the story of Cassiopeia and those of her family, list traits that are appropriate for each character. Make an effort to find a variety of adjectives, using a dictionary or thesaurus for assistance.

Cassiopeia

1. _____   3. _____   5. _____

2. _____   4. _____

Cepheus

1. _____   3. _____   5. _____

2. _____   4. _____

Andromeda

1. _____   3. _____   5. _____

2. _____   4. _____

Perseus

1. _____   3. _____   5. _____

2. _____   4. _____

Cetus

1. _____   3. _____   5. _____

2. _____   4. _____

Annotated Bibliography

Asimov, Isaac. *Astronomy in Ancient Times.* Milwaukee, WI: Gareth Stevens, 1995.
An updated version of the original, which contains short tales of ancient astronomy and includes fun-to-look-at illustrations.

———. *Folklore and Legends of the Universe.* Milwaukee, WI: Gareth Stevens, 1996.

Booth, David, comp. *'Til All the Stars Have Fallen: A Collection of Poems for Children.* New York: Puffin Books, 1989.
Contains a variety of nature poems.

Branley, Franklyn M. *The Big Dipper.* New York: HarperCollins, 1991.
A very simple picture book explaining the shape and location of the Big Dipper and the North Star.

———. *The Sky Is Full of Stars.* New York: HarperCollins, 1981.
A very simple picture book depicting several different constellations that can be seen at various times of the year. Gives directions for creating a constellation viewer.

Brenner, Barbara, ed. *The Earth Is Painted Green.* New York: Scholastic, 1994.
Consists of a variety of poems about nature.

Bruchac, Joseph, and Thomas Locker. *The Earth Under Sky Bear's Feet.* New York: Putnam and Grosset Group, 1995.
A variety of Native American nature poems.

Bruchac, Joseph, and Gayle Ross. *The Story of the Milky Way.* New York: Dial Books, 1995.
A Cherokee legend explaining how the stars came to be in the night sky.

Burke, Juliet Sharman, comp. *Stories from the Stars: An Abbeville Anthology.* New York: Abbeville, 1996.
Retellings of each of the zodiac constellation stories.

Chang, Cindy. *The Seventh Sister.* New York: Troll, 1994.
A delightful, colorful Chinese legend relating the tale of how the Milky Way came to be.

d'Aulaire, Ingri, and Edgar Parin d'Aulaire. *d'Aulaires' Book of Greek Myths.* New York: Doubleday, 1962.
A variety of Greek myths, including stories of all the major gods, simply retold for elementary-age students.

Esbensen, Barbara Juster, trans. *The Star Maiden.* New York: Little, Brown, 1988.
An Ojibway tale detailing the manner in which the stars became water lilies.

Fisher, Leonard Everett. *The Olympians.* New York: Holiday House, 1984.
Brief sketches of each of the major Greek gods.

Glow-in-the-Dark Constellations. Illuminations, 1994.
Besides the glow-in-the-dark constellations, this set contains a booklet of related myths and legends.

Goble, Paul. *Her Seven Brothers.* New York: Bradbury Press, 1988.

Hague, Michael. *The Book of Dragons.* New York: William Morrow, 1995.
A well-illustrated anthology of dragon tales from all over the world.

Hillman, Elizabeth. *Min-Yo and the Moon Dragon.* Orlando, FL: Harcourt Brace, 1992.
The story of how a little girl saves the Moon from falling by placing diamonds, which become the stars, in the sky.

Krupp, E. C. *The Big Dipper and You.* New York: Morrow Junior Books, 1989.
Relates ancient stories of the Big Dipper from all around the world using delightful illustrations. An excellent resource as well as an easy-to-read-and-understand book for students.

Langeler, Freddie. *Children of the Stars.* Oakland, CA: Amber Lotus/Kabouter Products, 1996.
An enchanting picture book that depicts stars as sky children lighting the world for the children of Earth. The story is told in verse.

Livingston, Myra Cohn. *Space Songs.* New York: Holiday House, 1988.
Original poems connected to all astronomy topics.

Low, Alice. *The Macmillan Book of Greek Gods and Heroes.* New York: Macmillan, 1985.
Retells simply many of the major Greek myths.

Lurie, Alison. *The Heavenly Zoo.* New York: Sunburst Books, 1996.
Animal constellation tales.

Mayo, Gretchen. *Star Tales: North American Indian Stories About the Stars.* Ontario: John Wiley, 1987.
North American Indian tales of various constellations.

Milford, Susan. *Tales of the Shimmering Sky.* Charlotte, NC: Williamson, 1996.
An outstanding children's book recounting various tales of the sky's natures; includes a wide range of hands-on activities.

Monjo, F. N. *The Drinking Gourd.* New York: HarperCollins, 1970.
The story of how escaped slaves used the North Star to travel north along the Underground Railroad.

Naden, C. J. *Perseus and Medusa.* Mahwah, NJ: Troll, 1981.
A simple picture book of how Perseus slays Medusa.

Osborne, Mary Pope. *Favorite Greek Myths.* New York: Scholastic, 1989.
Although this book retells some of the most popular Greek myths in a delightful way, be aware that the corresponding Roman names are used, rather than the Greek names.

Oughton, Jerrie. *How the Stars Fell Into the Sky.* Boston: Houghton Mifflin, 1992.
A Navajo legend depicting the manner in which stars came to be.

Palazzo-Craig, Janet, trans. *How Night Came to Be.* New York: Troll Communications, 1996.
A beginning legend retelling the Brazilian version of the difference between night and day.

Pearce, Q. L. *The Stargazers Guide to the Galaxy.* New York: Tom Doherty, 1991.
Contains illustrations of the major constellations along with brief descriptions of their mythological stories, how to find the stars, and star maps for all four seasons.

Russell, William. *Classic Myths to Read Aloud.* New York: Crown Trade, 1989.
Shortened versions of Greek myths appropriate for children.

Sessions, Larry. *Constellations.* Philadelphia: Running Press, 1993.
This is a miniature book that tells several constellation myths. Each myth and legend is retold from the point of view of three different cultures.

Simon, Seymour. *Space Words: A Dictionary.* New York: HarperCollins, 1991.

——. *Starwalk.* New York: William Morrow, 1995.
A collection of star-related poems written by others.

Snowden, Sheila. *The Young Astronomer.* Tulsa, OK: EDC, 1990.
An excellent resource for students and teachers with respect to all astronomy topics.

Trapani, Iza. *Twinkle, Twinkle Little Star.* Danvers, MA: Whispering Coyote Press, 1994.
The story of a little girl who spends the night traveling with a star. Based on the poem/song of the same name.

Vautier, Ghislaine, and Kenneth McLeish. *The Shining Stars*: *Greek Legends of the Zodiac*. New York: Cambridge University Press, 1981.

Simple, short stories retelling the legends of the zodiac constellations.

———. *The Way of the Stars: Greek Legends of the Constellations*. New York: Cambridge University Press, 1981.

Short retellings of various constellation stories.

References and Resources

Atwood, Ann. *Haiku: The Mood of the Earth*. New York: Charles Scribner's Sons, 1971.

———. *My Own Rhythm: An Approach to Haiku*. New York: Charles Scribner's Sons, 1973.

Haiku poetry and beautiful nature photographs to match. Inspiring books to share with students when introducing haiku poetry.

Darling, David J. *The Galaxies, Cities of Stars*. Minneapolis, MN: Dillon Press, 1995.

Freeman, Sara E. *Our Solar System: Ideas and Activities Across the Curriculum*. Palos Verdes Estates, CA: Frank Schaffer Publications, 1992.

Gustafson, John. *Stars, Clusters, and Galaxies*. New York: Simon & Schuster, 1992.

A good reference source for fourth- and fifth-graders, giving information about types of stars, the constellations, how to observe the night sky, and how to use a telescope.

Maynard, Christopher. *Stars and Planets: The Usborne Young Scientist*. New York: EDC, 1995.

Mitton, Jacqueline. *Dictionary of Astronomy*. New York: Penguin Books, 1993.

Ruiz, Andres Llamas. *Stars*. New York: Sterling, 1996.

Short and easy-to-understand explanations of all the different types of stars, as well as how a star begins. Visuals are colorful and complement the written explanations.

Schatz, Dennis, and Doug Cooper. *Astro Adventures*. Seattle, WA: Pacific Science Center, 1994.

Silverstein. Shel. *A Light in the Attic*. New York: Harper & Row, 1981.

Simon, Seymour. *Look Into the Night Sky*: *An Introduction to Star Watching*. New York: Viking Press, 1977.

Although this book is twenty years old, its content includes easy-to-read illustrations and explanations of the major stars and constellations. It is a good resource for beginning astronomy.

VanCleave, Janice. *Astronomy for Every Kid*. New York: John Wiley, 1991.

Simple science experiments for all astronomy-related topics.

———. *Constellations for Every Kid*. New York: John Wiley, 1997.

A variety of activities to assist in finding the constellations.

Musical Resources

Cooper, Don. *Star Tunes*. New York: Random House, 1991.

Delightful, catchy tunes dealing with all astronomy topics; consists of songbook and tape.

Glazer, Tom, and Dottie Evans. *Space Songs*. New York: Argosy Music Corp., 1959.

Songs that relay information about all astronomy topics.

Mauceri, John. *Journey to the Stars: A Sci-Fi Fantasy Adventure*. New York: Philips Classics Production, 1995.

Star Trek, *Star Wars*, and other science fiction music on compact disc.

Electronic Sources

BDM Federal, Inc. 1997. *NASA Observatorium*. 1995–97. URL: http://observe.ivv. nasa.gov/nasa/core.shtml (Accessed July 7, 1997).

Boschat, Mike. 1997. *Mike Boschat's Astronomy Page*. 1996. URL: http://www. atm.dal.ca/~andromed (Accessed July 7, 1997).

College of St. Benedict & St. John's University. 1997 *Tutorials for Astronomy*. 1996. URL: http://www.physics.csbsju. edu/astro (Accessed March, 1997). Click into "Constellations to Know."

Dolan, Chris. 1997. *Chris Dolan's Constellation Page*. 1995–97. URL: http://www.astro. wisc.edu/~dolan/constellations/ (Accessed March, 1997).
Stories and illustrations. Check Chris's homepage, too, for other astronomy links.

High-Energy Astrophysics Learning Center. 1997. URL: http://heasarc.gsfc.nasa. gov/docs/outreach.html (Accessed July 8, 1997).
Contains links to astronomy sources, an "Ask the Astronomer" section, and a "Teacher's Corner."

StarChild Team. 1997. *StarChild*. URL: http://heasarc.gsfc.nasa.gov/docs/ StarChild/StarChild.html (Accessed July 8, 1997).
Child-centered astronomy learning activities; two levels, ages 6–10 and 10–14.

Stone, Wes. 1997. *Sky Tour*. 1996–97. URL: http://www.lclark.edu/~wstone/ skytour/toc.html (Accessed July 8, 1997).
A tour of the sky consisting of all astronomy-related topics, including links to other resources.

CHAPTER 5

Traveling Through Space

Probably since the beginning of time, human beings have wondered about the mysteries of flight and outer space, and have asked, "What is it really like up there?" Most students are interested and fascinated by such a topic, so begin with some basics of the science of flight, rocketry, and gravity, and then take students through a timeline of space history, from the 1950s to the next century.

Flight

Flying and Fantasy

➤ *Literature: The Wing Shop*

Start an investigation of flight by displaying a variety of photographs or pictures depicting some common objects that fly and asking students to brainstorm their ideas about flying by completing the reproducible "My Ideas About Flight" (see page 129). Upon completion and discussion, read the short story *The Wing Shop*, and choose from any of these suggested follow-ups.

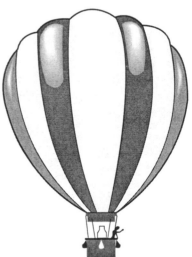

1. Have students formulate a list of items that fly, and then pretend that they have either acquired wings or some other aspect of the object that allows it to fly. Write a short story, paragraph, fairy tale, comic book page, etc., about the adventures that take place with this object's flying apparatus.

2. As a small-group project, have the group decide on a flying object. One person starts the adventure with a main idea sentence, passes the paper to the next person, who adds a detail to the paragraph, and so on around the group, until the paragraph(s) or stories are completed.

3. Review, through discussion, the messages *The Wing Shop* is trying to get across, the fantasy aspects of the story, and why is it that human beings were probably not meant to fly.

➤ *A Greek Myth: "Daedelus and Icarus"*

The Greek myth "Daedelus and Icarus" is a story that not only relates humankind's interest in flight, but expresses a human being's desire to be free by being able to fly like a bird. The story of Daedelus and Icarus can be found in the Greek myth books mentioned in Chapter 4; however, a beautifully illustrated picture book retelling this story is *Wings* by Jane Yolen.

Before reading this tale, have students complete and discuss numbers 1 and 2 on the reproducible, "My Ideas About Flight." Once students read the story, they should respond to number 3 and discuss the messages in the story, including their ideas about flight.

Flight Science

Once students have had an opportunity to think about flight, they need to investigate further. Use the bibliography at the end of this chapter and information from the Appendix to assist you in obtaining a variety of resources about flight from NASA, the Civil Air Patrol, and your local bookstore. Contact the public relations department of major airlines, a nearby airport, or large companies associated with the aircraft industry (Boeing, Lockheed Martin, etc.). If you have an air force base nearby or a recruiting office, people there may be willing to help out, as well.

An investigation of aerodynamics, the study of how air affects moving objects, should take place when studying flight science. This enables students to understand that air is actually *something*, contains weight, and has pressure. Refer to air experimentation ideas found in *Aviation Science Activities for Elementary Grades*.

From that point, have some fun with hot air balloons, using suggestions found in *History of Flight*, produced by the National Air and Space Museum, and *Aviation and Space Curriculum Guide, K–3*, provided by the FAA. As literature, *The Big Balloon Race*, a Reading Rainbow book, is a story that works well here.

Continue with the four forces of flight: lift, which allows an aircraft to get off the ground; gravity, which brings it back down; thrust, which moves it forward; and drag, which slows it down. Refer to the sources mentioned, as well as the following for more flight investigations involving hot air balloons and the four forces of flight: *Rocket Science*; *Flight: A Thematic Unit*; *Flight in the Atmosphere*; *175 Science Experiments*; *Air, Wind, and Flight*; and *Integrating Aerospace Science into the Curriculum: K–12*. There is much, much more to flight itself, as well as people throughout history associated with flight; however, for elementary-age students, knowledge of these basics provides good background for a unit on space travel, and encourages those with great interest to find out more.

Gravity

What Is It?

Mention the word *gravity*, and many students will immediately think of gravity's opposite, conjuring pictures of astronauts or aliens floating in space. Gravity is a very abstract concept, but again, some simple activities give students a basic idea of what it is all about. First, have students think and/or draw their thoughts about gravity, then work in pairs or small groups to discuss and record their reflections. Remind students that there should be no conversation about the correctness of ideas; all thoughts should be recorded. Have a class discussion and record the thoughts on a master list. Type the list, duplicate it for each student, and have each student decide which are true and which are false by writing a "T" or an "F" next to each statement. Save these statement sheets and complete the activity again after several gravity investigations.

How Does It Work?

Introduce students to Isaac Newton, the father of gravity, with the song "Gravity," from *Space Tunes*, and give students the opportunity to complete the "Falling Objects" experiment (see page 130). Gravity is the force that pulls all objects towards the center of the Earth (or other celestial body). This experiment demonstrates that gravity acts upon all objects equally when both objects hit the ground at the same time. Two experiments, "Paper Weight" and "Which Way Is Down?" from Janice VanCleave's book *Gravity*, will assist in understanding how gravity works.

Why Do I Weigh Less on the Moon Than on Earth?

Explain to students that their weight has to do with the strength of gravity, or downward force on their bodies, as well as the mass of their bodies. The force of gravity on Earth is equal to 1G, but because the force of gravity on the Moon is not as strong—six times less than what it is on Earth—their weight will be six times less. Students' mass, or the amount of matter their bodies have, only changes as they grow; so therefore, on any given day, their weight on the Moon would be less than on Earth. In contrast, the force of gravity on Jupiter is very strong; therefore students' weights would be greater. Refer to the chart in Chapter 3 (see page 75) that furnishes information on the force of gravity for each planet.

To illustrate further, take a picture of a polar bear (or even a small stuffed bear) and place it on a photo of Earth or on a globe. On Earth, a male polar bear weighs about 900 pounds. Place the polar bear on a picture of the Moon and indicate that the bear's weight would be six times less, or about 150 pounds, and with the polar bear on Jupiter, the bear's weight would be approximately 2600 pounds. The bear itself has not changed in any way, except to be somewhere that has a different force of gravity than on Earth.

For students to zestfully participate in determining their weight, or another object's weight, in various places in the universe, try the following activity.

1. Set up stations around the room by placing, on the floor, large photographs of the planets and the Moon, each marked with its g-force. Include calculators, a Post-it notepad, and a pencil.

2. In small groups, students may travel through the solar system, figuring their weights, marking their charts, and posting the information on the planet with the Post-it notes.

3. Because some students may feel uncomfortable about using their own weight, have students bring in small stuffed animals, find their Earth weights, and travel with them to the different planets, determining the stuffed animals' weights as they travel around the universe.

4. Each group should be assigned a celestial body for which to prepare a bar graph of the weights on that celestial body.

Check the bibliography for further information on activities dealing with mass, weight, and gravity.

Free Fall

The state of being *weightless*, as astronauts find themselves in space, excites students everywhere. Just the thought of being able to float around from place to place captures students' attention; however, there is a very scientific explanation for how and why this occurs. A zero-gravity situation occurs when two objects fall together. *Weight and Weightlessness*, by Franklyn Branley, and *Why Doesn't the Earth Fall Up?* by Vicki Cobb explain the concept of free fall very easily and clearly. The book by Mr. Branley, published in 1971, only shows cartoon drawings of space capsules, so this is also a good book to show students what space capsules looked like and how they returned to Earth. For older students, two excellent videotapes with teacher guides and experiments are available from NASA through your nearest TRC. Ask for *Newton in Space* and *Space Basics*, which are part of the Liftoff to Learning series.

Newton's Laws of Motion

A study of space science would not be complete without an investigation of rocketry and Newton's three laws of motion. The first law states that an object in motion will stay in motion in a straight line, unless it is acted upon by an outside force, and an object at rest will stay at rest, again, unless acted upon by an outside force. The second law states the mass of an object has an effect on its rate of acceleration and the force needed to move and stop the object. To get into space, massive objects, such as rockets and satellites, require a great deal of force and move slowly at launch. As the space vehicle burns fuel, and as in the case of the space shuttle, loses its solid rocket boosters, mass decreases and the vehicle accelerates more quickly. The third law refers to action-reaction, meaning that for every action, there is an equal, but opposite, reaction.

Isaac's First Law of Motion

Isaac Newton's first law of motion, as stated above, is also called the inertia principle. A simple demonstration could involve a ball rolled across the classroom. The ball will roll in a straight line until it is acted upon by another force, in this case, probably the classroom wall, will stop the ball from rolling. After this simple exhibition of inertia, ask students to come up with everyday situations in which inertia, or Newton's first law, can be confirmed.

Follow up with the "Egg Spin" experiment (see pages 131–32) adapted from *175 Science Experiments*, given as a family project home assignment. Provide a few days for students to do this, then schedule a classroom discussion, along with another performance of the experiment.

If you are willing, accompany this with the *magic trick* of pulling a tablecloth from underneath a set of china. Instead of the tablecloth and china, use a paper cup filled with a small amount of water and a paper towel or cloth. Place the cup on the edge of a desk with the cloth underneath and allow children to remove the cloth with a very quick pull. The cup should remain at rest as long as it was not acted upon by an outside force. It does work!

Isaac's Second Law of Motion

The second law of motion can be easily demonstrated using any two objects that are the same size, but have a different mass. An example would be two small plastic containers, such as margarine tubs, one empty and one full. Place these items on the classroom floor or a long table. Using a hair dryer at low speed, force the empty container to move. Note how easily and quickly it moves. Do the same with the full container. Does it move with the dryer on low speed? high speed? Do you need to use more than one hair dryer? What is the rate of acceleration?

Students can also throw objects into the air noting differences in force required to throw and catch each one. A tennis ball and same-size Styrofoam ball work well, as do golf balls and Ping-Pong balls. Follow up by having students brainstorm some everyday situations that exhibit Newton's second law of motion.

Isaac's Third Law of Motion

Although all of Newton's laws play a part in aerospace science, this one is easily observable when launching rockets. A simple demonstration for action/reaction is to blow up a balloon and let it go without tying it. Before letting go of the balloon, students will be able to tell you, of course, what will happen; but ask them to observe carefully which way the air travels and which way the balloon travels. The air goes backward out of the balloon, while the balloon moves forward. The action is the air moving out and the reaction is the forward motion of the balloon.

After demonstrating action/reaction, have students brainstorm everyday situations that follow this third law of motion, and then participate in the "Rocket Balloons" activity (see pages 133–34).

Newton, Rockets, and Reader's Theatre

Two short dramatizations, located in *Great Moments in Science: Experiments and Readers Theatre*, that unite language arts and science are "Apple, Moons and Questions," which relates the story of Isaac Newton's discovery of gravity, and "Launching a Scientist," the story of how Robert Goddard undertook the task of developing rockets. Each of these short plays are accompanied by science experiments dealing with the respective scientific concepts.

In addition, for further information on rocket activities and examining Newton's Laws of Motion, make use of NASA's teacher guide *Rockets: A Teacher's Guide with Activities in Science, Mathematics, and Technology*, available through the NASA TRC. An excellent source for the history of rockets used in U.S. manned missions is *The U.S. Space Camp Book of Rockets*.

Space History

Most students today view space travel in a couple of different ways—either through the space shuttle, which looks more like an airplane than a spacecraft, or through the science fiction of *Star Wars* or *Star Trek*. A study of space history will develop students' knowledge of how it all began, and how different it was when space travel originated in the 1950s.

A Space History Interview

Have students begin by interviewing a family member or other acquaintance who remembers space travel history as it was in the late 1950s and throughout the 1960s using the "Space History Interview" sheet provided (see pages 135–36). Students may wish to record the interviews to be played back in class, or, if there is someone you or a student knows that is particularly knowledgeable, invite that person to come in and visit with the class.

When the interviews have been completed, be prepared to view some photos of space travel history. A good source for space history photographs, along with reproducible activities, is *Discovery*, a booklet produced by NASA and the National Air and Space Museum.

Compile the information from the interviews on a class chart, a sample of which is given on page 122. Divide the class into groups based on the chart categories. To organize and display the information, have each group make a staged rocket. This can be done by cutting squares (about 10 by 10 inches) of construction paper, writing one piece of information on each square, taping the squares together, and topping it off with a triangle or rocket-shaped piece of construction paper containing the name of the category, date, and the group members' names.

A Space History Museum

Once students have been introduced to the "ancient" world of space travel, have them consider further research and the idea of creating museum-like displays that exhibit their new knowledge. Have students select from the following topics:

➢ The 1950s unmanned satellites

➢ Animal research for spaceflight

➢ The Mercury Program

➢ The Gemini Program

➢ The Apollo Program

➢ Skylab (1970s)

➢ Types of rockets used in the 1960s to launch the spacecraft

- ➢ Unmanned exploration in the 1960s

- ➢ Mission patches

- ➢ Astronauts

- ➢ Scientists involved in developing various aspects of early space travel

- ➢ Russian spaceflight

- ➢ Other topics of choice

Students should plan their research by composing questions that focus on students' interests and inquiries on the topic; however, encourage the inclusion of questions related to time periods, types of rockets, purposes of missions, types of spacecraft, people involved, etc.

  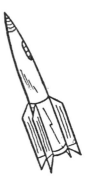 

➤ *Museum Display Suggestions*

Upon completion of the research, students should prepare a display of their findings for their museum exhibit. During school year 1996–97, my fourth-grade class designed a variety of projects for an interactive space fair, some of which are detailed here.

To provide information on the Galileo spacecraft exploring Jupiter, Elyse and Jessica created a kid-size spacecraft with a window on top. Students would enter the spacecraft, listen to a recording made by Jessica and Elyse enumerating facts about Jupiter and the Galileo spacecraft, and then respond to questions shown to them on a card through the spacecraft window.

The Space Station Race was designed by Jacky and James. Two 1-meter sticks were placed side-by-side on a wall and consisted of pieces of Velcro placed at various intervals. Upside-down Styrofoam cups, with attached pieces of Velcro, were used as the space station replicas. Two students were provided with information about the space station, and then were required to answer questions. If a question was answered correctly, the paper cup space station would be moved up a notch on the meter stick belonging to the student who answered, and the first "space station" to get to the top was the winner.

Other project possibilities include: simple board games, an electronic quiz board (*Inventions: Thematic Unit* by Teacher Created Materials explains how to make one), a board with information windows and flip-up covers, models of spacecraft and/or items that represent a portion of space history along with written explanations of what is on display, quiz games, etc. Offer suggestions to get students started, but they are generally pretty good at coming up with their own ideas.

➤ *Patch Design*

During the process of completing the research and museum displays, have the class decide on a name for the museum and design a space patch to represent the class project and the museum name. Each of the research groups may want to design a patch to represent their individual topics and displays, as well.

To give students an idea of what to include on their patches, have them observe NASA mission patches, examples of which can be found at http://www.hq.nasa.gov/office/pao/History/mission_patches.html (as of August 8, 1997). Mission patches generally have the name and number of the mission, the names of the astronauts, and a graphic that represents some aspect of the mission's purpose. In fact, when taking note of the patches, present students with the opportunity to guess each mission's purpose based on the design. Perhaps a pair of students would be interested in researching particular missions, their patches, and developing a museum display on that topic. Photographs of patches through and including the Skylab program can be found in *All We Did Was Fly to the Moon*, along with explanations of patch designs, nicknames for spacecraft and missions, and how the astronauts eventually won permission to have input into each of their missions' patch designs.

➤ *Museum Presentation*

When all projects have been completed, set a date and time for display, design invitations, and send them to parents and other classes. Past experience has taught me to have classes spend about a half-hour in the museum, and have my own class present for only a couple of hours, as the students (and their teacher) do become somewhat fatigued. Try to plan two half-day sessions for presentation, rather than one full day. I once had a fifth-grade class that was so tired following a museum presentation, they requested a nap time. Students did take advantage of the half-hour allotted to them for such an activity that day.

➤ *A Different Type of Timeline*

For each portion of space history, have students design a shoe box timeline in which a scene from a section in space history is designed and placed in a shoe box. Place the top on the shoe box, decorate the box accordingly, and cut a large hole in the box so that others may peer at the space history scene. An index card on the top or side of the shoe box should briefly summarize the scene. Line up the shoe boxes in timeline order and allow students to take a peek into space history.

STS: Space Transportation System

Once the U.S. had accomplished the task of going to the Moon, and keeping astronauts in space for a relatively long period of time during the Skylab project, what could be next? Well, Mars is always available, a return to the Moon could be a possibility, and there are endless space explorations of all types, but how could it be done and at a reasonable cost?

The Space Transportation System (better know as the space shuttle) was designed to be a reusable transport system into space for scientific data collection, and to attempt to establish a permanent presence in space by building a space station. For the most part, it has done the first two, and although somewhat behind schedule, NASA and other countries of the world are in the process of setting the stage for the international space station. Let's take a look at how the shuttle works, what it is like to live and work on the shuttle, and what purposes it has and will serve.

The Shuttle: How It Works

➤ Background Information

The shuttle system is made up of three main parts: the orbiter, the solid rocket boosters, and the external tank. The orbiter is the part in which the astronauts live, and it houses the payload bay for carrying cargo, such as satellites, or the Spacelab, with which astronauts conduct various types of experiments. The solid rocket boosters (SRBs) are the two rockets on either side of the orbiter, contain solid fuel, and once their fuel is used, are jettisoned into the ocean to be picked up by navy ships and prepared for use on another shuttle launch. The giant middle tank is the liquid fuel tank known as ET or the external tank. It contains liquid hydrogen, is not reusable, and powers the orbiter's main engines. Once its fuel is used, the ET is jettisoned and breaks up into small pieces that fall into the Indian Ocean. The orbiter then relies on its two maneuvering control systems to orbit the Earth.

➤ Summarizing Shuttle Facts

To interest students in the operation of the space shuttle, introduce the book *How to Fly the Space Shuttle*. If you are able to do so, obtain several copies, enabling students to work on the "Space Shuttle Task Cards" provided at the end of this chapter (see pages 137–38). To prepare, place a copy of the book in a folder with a task card and the materials needed to complete the assignment. Read aloud to students pages 1, 2, and 4 to spark their interest, and then allow students to work on the task folders at designated times.

For task card 1 you will need to use page 2.30 from *Space Shuttle: Activities for Primary and Intermediate Students* for the cut-and-paste activity. For task card 2, develop a vocabulary worksheet using context for the following words:

avalanche	console
thrust	abort
throttle	optimum
acceleration	efficiently
monitoring	contingency
gauge	

For task card 3, you may want to consider making a chart of NASA acronyms for the classroom, or just place the acronyms on 5-by-8-inch index cards with their meanings, and hang them randomly around the classroom.

After discovering how the shuttle operates for launch, allow students to continue following the mission in *How to Fly the Space Shuttle* by creating your own task cards for the remainder of the book, or use it for a re-creation of a class shuttle mission.

Living in Space

This is a topic that generates a lot of student interest. For an introduction, use the "My One-Day Activity List" (see pages 139–41) and have students keep track, either on a school day or weekend day, of all things they do. Next to each item, have them write how they think that activity would be either different or impossible if they were spending time on the space shuttle. When the assignment has been completed, review it with students and compile a list of questions students have about living in space. Resources that are especially helpful are:

> *A Day in Space*
>
> *How Do You Go to the Bathroom in Space?*
>
> *To Space and Back*
>
> *The Space Shuttle Operator's Manual*
>
> *If You Were an Astronaut*
>
> *I Want to Be an Astronaut*
>
> *Human Spaceflight: Activities for the Intermediate Student*
>
> *Living in Space: Books I and II*

As students are finding answers to their living-in-space questions, supplement their research and maintain their interest by doing some activities.

➤ *Communication Skills*

Astronauts often need to communicate with ground control personnel, receiving instructions for completing an experiment or repairing an object without benefit of visual aids. This task can be made more difficult if instructions are not given and/or received properly. Give students practice communicating instructions with the following activity.

Each pair of students should be given a small plastic bag containing centimeter cubes, tangram pieces, or pattern blocks, and student pairs should sit on the floor, back to back, so that neither student can see what the other is doing. The first student should use cubes to build an object or create a design and then verbally instruct the second student how to build the same exact object—same shapes, same positions, same colors, etc. Partners should take turns for building/instructing, and you will probably find that students need to practice this several times. Most students find it a challenge, and it is a good activity throughout the school year as a simple free-time exercise.

➤ *Astronaut for a Day*

Most clothing the astronauts wear during launch, landing, and in orbit contains many pockets for storing items such as pens, scissors, notebooks, etc. Velcro strips on the outside of clothing are helpful for stashing items while in use so the tools do not float away.

Have students come to school one day prepared to go through the day as astronauts. You will probably need to send home a note ahead of time asking for parents' help in the preparation. Suggest that all items to be used that day, such as pencils, papers, books, etc., be stored in a lunchbox, pencil box, backpack, etc. No item may be left on top or inside of desks; otherwise it will float away. Students should come dressed in clothing that contains many pockets and/or Velcro strips. Place Velcro strips on pencils, erasers, etc., so that when students do use them, they can position them on their clothing or inside the pockets. Have students use clipboards to hold paper. When using books or clipboards, caution students to hold onto them so they do not float away. In addition, propose that students sponge bathe that day and swallow their toothpaste when they brush their teeth. Hopefully, parents will be willing to go along for just one day.

➤ Eating in Space

See the "Space Food" reproducible for this activity (pages 142–43), and request that students bring in bowls, plastic drinking cups, and spoons.

➤ Additional Living-in-Space Activities

For more living-in-space ideas, use the *Living in Space Books* that are available from your regional NASA TRC. These books consist of living-in-the-orbiter activities, spacelab activities, and additional communication activities. Try to obtain and view Imax videos such as *The Dream Is Alive* or *Destiny in Space*, which portray living in space.

Space Future

As this book was being written, the Hubble space telescope had recently been upgraded and was sending back phenomenal images of the universe; Pathfinder had landed on Mars, providing photos beyond many people's wildest imaginations; the Cassini spacecraft was being prepared to embark toward a rendezvous with Saturn; and NASA was primed to launch the beginning segments of the international space station, Alpha. The past forty years have seen quite a bit of WOWS in space exploration, but there are still plenty of WOWS to discover and explore, and, hopefully, our students will be ready and willing to participate.

The International Space Station

Freedom was the original name of the space station proposed by NASA and a few international space agencies; however, in 1994, the space station was redesigned to include additional international space agencies and make the station a bit more compact. The result is space station Alpha, and once it is assembled, it will include segments provided by Russia, Japan, Canada, the European Space Agency, and the United States. The station will be built during approximately seventy-three U.S. space shuttle and Russian missions over about five to six years, beginning in 1998. The space station will orbit the Earth and hold a crew of six, who will spend several months at a time completing science investigations.

Building a Space Station

As the many space shuttle flights take place, and the astronauts put the sections of the space station together, students may be interested in building their own space station. Consider these suggestions.

1. Review the Skylab missions of the 1970s and obtain photos of artists' renditions of the space station that are available through your NASA TRC. Have students become familiar with the various segments of the station, information which can be found on the back of the photos. The website http://station.nasa.gov/index-m.html is also a helpful source of information. Be sure to discuss the truss structures of the space station, the reason they are needed, and involve students in experimenting with sunlight and solar panels.

2. Next, have students work in groups to design a station using materials that are readily accessible at home or at school.

3. Rather than have each group design its own station, design a class station, and have each group represent a segment of the station and be responsible for building that part.

4. If you prefer, specific directions for building a space station can be found in *Odyssey* magazine's December 1995 issue, "Docking in Space." This issue of the magazine also furnishes information about the segments of the space station, as well as how the shuttle currently docks with the Russian Mir space station.

5. Students may also be interested in constructing a kid-sized habitat module, which can become a learning center for completing science activities.

Science Fiction and the Space Station

While obtaining information and building a space station, read aloud portions of Jules Verne's imaginary journeys to students (some of which you may find in children's versions). When students have completed their space station, they may want to plan and write the story of their own visionary excursions, either as scientists aboard the station, as travelers elsewhere in the universe, or as the discoverers of life elsewhere.

Other pieces of science fiction literature available for students are *Stinker from Space*, *Stinker's Return*, *Alistair in Outer Space*, *Alistair and the Alien Invasion*, *Space Rock*, *Moog-Moog: Space Barber*, *Spaceburger*, and *Spacey Riddles*. After reading *Spaceburger*, students may wish to design their own restaurants, supermarkets, or department stores that would have an outer space theme. Students could write and illustrate their own space riddles based on all they have learned during a space travel unit, or create their own alien adventures, as in the Alistair or Stinker books. In addition, students may wish to consider using the good and evil aspects of fairy tales to write their own fairy tale space adventure.

Other writing and literature response activities might include a letter back to Earth describing life on the space station; a musical special made for television based on life aboard the space station; a vacation plan for travel from the space station to somewhere else in the universe (where, when, things to do, packing needs, etc.); a version of an original space exploration experience as it would be written in a history textbook by a historian, and/or editorialize about the adventure.

Whatever area of space travel you and your students decide to focus upon, I hope that all will have a safe and exciting mission.

My Ideas About Flight

Name _____ Date _____

1. When I look at a bird fly, I notice

   a. _____

   b. _____

   c. _____

   d. _____

2. If I hold a piece of paper flat, away from my body and let it fall, I notice

   a. _____

   b. _____

   c. _____

   d. _____

3. Based on my observations, these are some ideas I have about what allows an object to fly:

   a. _____

   b. _____

   c. _____

   d. _____

Falling Objects

Name _____ Date _____

Materials needed: a basketball and a tennis ball, or two Nerf balls, one large and one small

Procedure:
a.   Hold your arms straight out in front of you, with both arms at the same height and even with your shoulders.

b.   Hold the basketball in one hand, and the tennis ball in the other.

c.   Make a prediction. When you drop both balls at exactly the same time, which one will hit the ground first?

_____

Explain why you think so.

_____

_____

d.   Drop both balls at exactly the same time, and have a partner watch to see which ball hits the ground first.

1.   Follow the procedure at least three times.

What happened the first time you dropped the balls?

_____

_____

What happened the second time?

_____

_____

What happened the third time?

_____

_____

2.   Based on the results of this experiment, can you make a statement about gravity? What is it?

_____

_____

_____

_____

The Egg Spin

Name _____ Date _____

Materials needed: one raw egg
                           one hard-boiled egg
                           a large paper plate

1. First Procedure: First you will be spinning each egg, one at a time, on the plate and observing how each one spins, how it stops, and when it stops. What do you think you will notice as the raw egg spins and then stops?

_____

_____

What about the hard-boiled egg? Will its spinning motion be different than that of the raw egg? Will the cooked egg stop quickly or take more time to do so?

_____

_____

Now spin the raw egg on the plate. Record what you observe of the egg's spinning motion, how it stops, and when it stops.

_____

_____

Do the same with the hard-boiled egg and record your observations.

_____

_____

2. Second Procedure: This time, as you spin each egg, you will quickly stop the spinning motion by placing your hand on top of the egg. As you do this with the raw egg, what do you think will happen?

_____

_____

From *Soaring Through the Universe*. © 1999 Joanne C. Letwinch. Teacher Ideas Press. (800) 237-6124.

What about the hard-boiled egg? As the egg spins and is quickly stopped, what do you think you will observe?

_____

_____

Now follow this procedure. Spin the raw egg on the plate, quickly place your hand on top of the egg to stop it from spinning, and immediately let go. What happens?

_____

_____

Do exactly the same thing with the hard-boiled egg and record your observations.

_____

_____

3. Do this experiment several times to see if your results are the same each time. Are the results for the raw egg the same or different? Explain.

_____

_____

4. Are the results for the hard-boiled egg the same or different? Explain.

_____

_____

5. What do these results have to do with inertia?

_____

_____

_____

_____

_____

Rocket Balloons

Name _____ Date _____

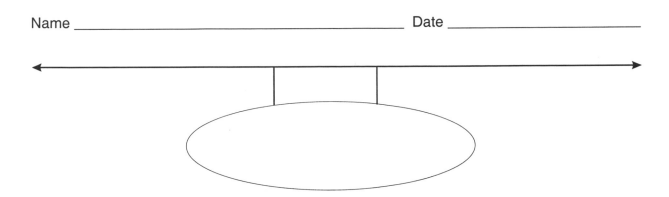

This experiment works best when students work in pairs or groups of three.

Materials needed for each group:
- two to four long balloons, although the 8-inch size works well
- fishing line or very thin string, at least a meter long
- one large straw
- masking tape

Procedure:
- Tie one end of the string to a chair and slip the straw through the other end. Pull the string tight and tie it to another chair so that the string is in a straight line.

- Place the two pieces of masking tape to the bottom of the straw, blow up the balloon, and using the masking tape, attach it to the straw while being careful not to allow air to escape from the balloon.

- After a 5-4-3-2-1 countdown, launch the rocket by letting go of the balloon. Which way did the balloon move and why? Which way did the air go? How does this demonstrate Newton's Third Law of Motion?

- Complete the "Rocket Balloon Record Sheet" and devise other rocket balloon experiments, being very careful to change only one variable (size of balloon, length of string, how the string is held [up, down, straight across], etc.).

- Record the results.

From *Soaring Through the Universe*. © 1999 Joanne C. Letwinch. Teacher Ideas Press. (800) 237-6124.

Rocket Balloon Record Sheet

Name _____ Date _____

Experiment #	Size of Balloon	Length of String	Position of String	Other Variable	Results

Space History Interview

Name of student _____

Name of person interviewed _____

Date interviewed _____

1. What is the name of the Russian unmanned satellite that was launched on October 4, 1957?

   _____

2. When did the U.S. launch its first unmanned satellite and what was its name?

   _____

3. Was a Russian cosmonaut or American astronaut launched into space first?

   _____

4. Who was the first cosmonaut in space? _____

5. Who was the first astronaut in space? _____

6. What do you know about the Mercury (one-man spacecraft) program in the early 1960s?

   _____

   _____

   _____

   _____

7. What do you know about the Gemini (two-man spacecraft) program in the mid-1960s?

   _____

   _____

   _____

   _____

8. What do you know about the Apollo (three-man spacecraft) program in the late 1960s?

_____

_____

_____

_____

9. How were space vehicles different during the 1960s than they are today?

_____

_____

_____

_____

10. How was space travel different during the 1960s than it is today?

_____

_____

_____

_____

11. My own questions.

_____

_____

_____

_____

_____

_____

_____

_____

Space Shuttle Task Card # 1

1. Read the purple section on page 4. On page 5, look at the picture that shows the parts of the space shuttle.

2. Shuttle parts—Cut and Paste Activity. Complete this activity and label each segment of the shuttle.

3. Cut out the following cards. Write the answer to each question on each card and glue the cards around the space transportation system picture that was completed in step 2.

What are the three main parts of the space transportation system?

a. _____

b. _____

c. _____

What are the two reusable parts of the space transportation system?

a. _____

b. _____

What are the three ways that make the orbiter different than any other spacecraft?

a. _____

b. _____

c. _____

Space Shuttle Task Card # 2

1. Vocabulary worksheet.

2. Read the white pages, 8–19.

3. You will be listing the steps for liftoff. Using the flashcards provided in this folder, write the steps for liftoff, one on each card until all steps have been listed.

4. On a 12-by-18-inch piece of construction paper, place the steps for liftoff in the proper order and add illustrations.

Space Shuttle Task Card # 3

1. NASA uses a lot of acronyms (words formed from the first letters of each word in a phrase or title). NASA itself is an acronym meaning **N**ational **A**eronautics and **S**pace **A**dministration.

2. *How to Fly the Space Shuttle* contains many acronyms. In the pages you have read so far, find as many acronyms as possible.

3. On a separate piece of paper, make a list of the acronyms and their meanings. Add illustrations if you like.

Space Shuttle Task Card # 4

Choices:

1. As you read pages 1–19, you can probably sense that the author is having many different feelings. Make a poster of faces that express the feelings you think the author is experiencing. Label the emotion. Tell at what point during the liftoff adventure the author seems to have that particular feeling.

2. Rewrite pages 1–19 as a skit and perform it for the class. Add appropriate music.

3. Pages 1–19 are full of similes. Find them and make an illustrated simile booklet.

My One-Day Activity List

Name _____ Date _____

Time	Earth Activity	Difference in Activity During Spaceflight
A.M. 8:00–9:00		
9:00–10:00		
10:00–11:00		
11:00–12:00		
P.M. 12:00–1:00		
1:00–2:00		

Time	Earth Activity	Difference in Activity During Spaceflight
2:00–3:00		
3:00–4:00		
4:00–5:00		
5:00–6:00		
6:00–7:00		
7:00–8:00		
8:00–9:00		
9:00 until morning		

Illustration of what my Earth activities might look like during spaceflight:

Space Food

Name _____ Date _____

Fun Food Fact # 1

Mercury astronauts ate food that was prepared as bite-sized cubes. Sometimes their food looked like toothpaste because the food was put into and eaten from aluminum tubes. Astronauts did not think this food was very tasty.

Fun Food Activity # 1—Eating Like a Mercury Astronaut

    a. Put some applesauce in a small plastic bag and seal it tightly.

    b. With a pair of scissors, snip off a corner at the bottom of the bag and eat the applesauce.

Fun Food Fact # 2

Scientists slowly improved the way food could be stored and eaten during spaceflight. Skylab even had a refrigerator and a freezer.

Fun Food Fact # 3

Space shuttle astronauts now have a lot of food choices. All food that needs to be cooked and prepared is done so beforehand and stored in different ways so that no refrigeration is needed. Weight must be considered when packing food for a space shuttle mission. For certain foods, as much water as possible is removed. Each item of food is then individually packed.

Astronauts eat these *rehydratable* foods and beverages: scrambled eggs, soup, and shrimp cocktail, by adding water to the packaging. If heating is necessary, the convection oven on board the space shuttle is used.

Fun Food Activity # 2—Enjoying Rehydratable Food

    a. Place cornflakes and powdered milk in a plastic bag.

    b. Weigh the bag.

    c. Rehydrate the bag with water and shake.

    d. Weigh the bag.

    e. What is the difference in weight?

    f. Use a spoon to eat breakfast like an astronaut.

Fun Food Fact # 4

Some food on the space shuttle is *intermediate moisture food*, which means a small amount of water is left in so the food stays soft. Fruits are an example of this type of food.

Fun Food Activity # 3—Enjoying Intermediate Moisture Food

    a.   Take a medium-sized apple, pear, or peach and weigh it.

    b.   Cut the fruit into six pieces and place it on a paper towel for a few days. As moisture leaves the fruit, the fruit will dry up. (Keep food lightly covered with wax paper to avoid bacteria.)

    c.   Weigh the dried fruit.

    d.   What is the weight difference?

    e.   Now you can eat fruit as an astronaut would.

Fun Food Fact # 5

Some foods eaten by astronauts, such as raisins, nuts, granola bars, and bread, are eaten in their *natural form*, so enjoy some natural-form food just as an astronaut would.

(Smith, 1988)

Annotated Bibliography

Baird, Anne. *The U.S. Space Camp Book of Rockets*. New York: Morrow Junior Books, 1994.
An excellent history of the rockets used for U.S. manned spaceflight.

Branley, Franklyn M. *Rockets and Satellites*. New York: Harper & Row, 1987.
Explains how satellites and rockets get into and stay in orbit around the Earth.

———. *Weight and Weightlessness*. New York: Thomas Y. Crowell, 1971.
Mr. Branley makes this difficult-to-grasp concept a little bit easier to understand.

Buller, Jon, and Susan Schade. *Space Rock*. New York: Random House, 1988.

Campbell, Peter A. *Launch Day*. Brookfield, WI: Millbrook Press, 1995.
A picture book that tells a story of how the shuttle and the astronauts are prepared for launch.

Cobb, Vicki. *Why Doesn't the Earth Fall Up?* New York: Lodestar Books, 1988.
Excellent explanations of all of Newton's laws with amusing pencil drawings.

Coerr, Eleanor. *The Big Balloon Race*. New York: Harper & Row, 1981.
About a little girl who accidentally gets involved in a hot air balloon adventure. Good for early elementary grades.

"Docking in Space." *Odyssey* (December 1995).
An issue devoted to the MIR and the international space station.

Douty, Esther. *The Brave Balloonists: America's First Airmen*. Champaign, IL: Garrard, 1974.
The first story in this book recounts the story of the first balloon flight in North America during revolutionary times.

Fradin, Dennis B. *Skylab: A New True Book*. Chicago: Childrens Press, 1984.
The story of Skylab.

Hall, Katy, and Lisa Eisenberg. *Spacey Riddles*. New York: Dial Books, 1992.

Hosking, Wayne. *Flights of Imagination: An Introduction to Aerodynamics*. Washington, DC: National Science Teachers Association, 1990.
An excellent series of activities for a beginner's study of aerodynamics.

Lattimer, Richard. *All We Did Was Fly to the Moon*. Alachua, FL: The Whispering Eagle Press, 1983.
A brief history of the U.S. race to the Moon, from Mercury through the Skylab program. A very good resource for students that includes interesting anecdotes and insignia information.

Lord, Suzanne, and Jolie Epstein. *A Day in Space*. New York: Scholastic, 1986.
A picture book, good for grades 2–4, explaining what it is like to live on the space shuttle for a day.

Marko, Katherine McGlade. *Animals in Orbit*. New York: Franklin Watts, 1991.
The story of the Soviet cosmonaut dogs and the U.S. monkeys and chimps used to test spaceflight prior to human spaceflight. Wonderful to use for debating the pros and cons of animal use in science.

Maze, Stephanie. *I Want to Be an Astronaut*. New York: Harcourt Brace, 1997.
A beginner's book on all aspects of spaceflight containing beautiful NASA photographs.

Moche, Dinah L. *The Astronauts*. New York: Random House, 1978.

———. *Astronomy Today*. New York: Random House, 1992.
Contains a well-done graphic and verbal explanation of a space shuttle launch and landing, as well as details about the orbiter.

———. *If You Were an Astronaut*. Racine, WI: Western, 1985.
A simple picture book about life as an astronaut.

Myring, Lynn. *Finding Out About Rockets and Spaceflight*. Tulsa, OK: EDC, 1991.

Simple explanations and graphics of various types of space vehicles.

Pinkwater, Daniel. *Spaceburger: A Kevin Spoon and Mason Mintz Story*. New York: Macmillan, 1993.

Science fiction story, appropriate for early readers.

Pogue, William R. *How Do You Go to the Bathroom in Space?* New York: Tom Doherty, 1991.

Written by a former Skylab astronaut, this book has a question-and-answer format relating information on just about everything involving spaceflight.

Ride, Sally, and Susan Okie. *To Space and Back*. New York: William Morrow, 1986.

Describing a space shuttle mission from launch to landing, a well-written book for students containing fabulous NASA photographs.

Sadler, Marilyn. *Alistair and the Alien Invasion*. New York: Simon & Schuster, 1994.

Another of Alistair's science fiction adventures.

———. *Alistair in Outer Space*. New York: Prentice Hall Press, 1984.

An amusing science fiction story of a young boy's visit to outer space.

Scholastic Voyages of Discovery: The Story of Flight. New York: Scholastic, 1995.

An excellent book that describes how a variety of objects fly. Comes with a teacher's guide, too.

Seller, Mick. *Air, Wind, and Flight*. New York: Aladdin Books, 1992.

All types of easy-to-do flight science experiments.

Service, Pamela F. *Stinker from Space*. New York: Charles Scribner's Sons, 1988.

A good science fiction story for upper elementary students.

———. *Stinker's Return*. New York: Charles Scribner's Sons, 1993.

A sequel to *Stinker from Space*.

Shorto, Russell. *How to Fly the Space Shuttle*. New York: W. W. Norton, 1992.

A fictional space shuttle flight told from the point of view of the author who seems to be on the flight by mistake. Very amusing and full of space shuttle facts.

Teague, Mark. *Moog-Moog: Space Barber*. New York: Scholastic, 1990.

West, Ruth Gold. *Why Does It Fly?* Paoli, PA: Project Packet Press, 1990.

A variety of flying objects, such as gliders, a Wright flyer, and boomerangs, with which to experiment.

Wiese, Jim. *Rocket Science*. New York: John Wiley, 1995.

All types of physical science experiments, including air, water, magnetism, and mechanics.

Woodruff, Elvira. *The Wing Shop*. New York: Holiday House, 1991.

A delightful story of a little boy who has moved to a new neighborhood and tries to fly back to visit his old community.

Yolen, Jane. *Wings*. Orlando, FL: Harcourt Brace, 1991.

The beautifully retold and illustrated adventure of Daedelus and Icarus's attempt to fly.

References and Resources

Andrews, Sheila Briskin, and Audrey Kirschenbaum. *Living in Space: Books I and II*. Washington, DC: NASA, 1987.

Arnold, H. J. P., ed. *Man in Space: An Illustrated History of Space Flight*. New York: SMITHMARK, 1993.

Includes information on the Russian space station, MIR, as well as all of space history. Terrific photographs.

Aviation and Space Curriculum Guide, K–3. Washington, DC: U.S. Department of Transportation, 1992.

Aviation Science Activities for Elementary Grades. Washington, DC: U.S. Department of Transportation.

Bondurant, Lynn R. Jr. *On the Wings of a Dream: The Space Shuttle.* Washington, DC: National Air and Space Museum, 1988.
One of my favorite resources for information about the space shuttle, this booklet has excellent graphics, photographs, and easy-to-understand information for students.

Canright, Shelley. *Aeronautic Adventure: An Earth-Space Investigation Designed for Elementary Students.* Hampton, VA: NASA Langley Research Center, 1986.
There is a video that goes along with this.

Destiny in Space. 40 min. Imax, 1994. Videocassette.
Includes scenes of astronauts working and living in space and the space shuttle orbiting the Earth. (See Appendix for address.)

Discovery. Washington, DC: NASA Education Division, 1994.
All types of activities regarding the science of flight, especially geared for K–3 students.

The Dream Is Alive. 37 min. Imax, 1985. Videocassette.
Earlier footage, but no less dramatic than *Destiny in Space*, of astronauts living and working on the space shuttle.

Goldfluss, Karen J., and Patricia Miriani Sima. *Inventions: Thematic Unit.* Huntington Beach, CA: Teacher Created Materials, 1993.

Hartsfield, John W. *History of Flight: Activities for the Primary Student.* Cleveland, OH: NASA Lewis Research Center, 1982.
No experiments, but a variety of language and math puzzles regarding the history of flight.

———. *Human Spaceflight: Activities for the Intermediate Student.* Cleveland, OH: NASA Lewis Research Center, 1985.
Covers all areas of spaceflight from the beginning to the present.

Hartsfield, John W., and Shirley Norlem. *Space Shuttle: Activities for Primary and Intermediate Students.* Cleveland, OH: NASA Lewis Research Center, 1987.
Contains a variety of fact sheets about living on the space shuttle as well as language and math activities.

Haven, Kendall. *Great Moments in Science: Experiments and Readers Theatre.* Englewood, CO: Teacher Ideas Press, 1996.
Dramatizations of various scientists and their discoveries, the book includes experiments designed to complement each of the skits.

History of Flight. Washington, DC: National Air and Space Museum, 1988.
Includes background information for teachers and integrated activities.

Joels, Kerry Mark, and Gregory P. Kennedy. *The Space Shuttle Operator's Manual.* New York: Random House, 1988.
Everything you wanted to know and wanted to ask about the space shuttle and living and operating in space.

Kerrod, Robin. *The Illustrated History of NASA: Anniversary Edition.* New York: Gallery Books, 1988.
Includes information regarding early rocketry, the Soviet Union's initial space successes, and all of U.S. spaceflight up to and including the Challenger disaster. Loaded with NASA photographs.

Liftoff to Learning: Newton in Space. 13 min. NASA, 1992. Videocassette and resource guide.
Explains Newton's laws and how they apply to space travel.

Liftoff to Learning: Space Basics. 21 min. NASA, 1991. Videocassette and resource guide.
The basics of launch, orbit, microgravity, and landing the space shuttle.

Ray, Robert D., and Joan Klingel Ray. *Integrating Aerospace Science into the Curriculum: K–12.* Englewood, CO: Teacher Ideas Press, 1992.

Rockets: A Teacher's Guide with Activities in Science, Mathematics, and Technology. Washington, DC: NASA, 1996.

Schmidt, Carolyn E. *Challenges for Space Explorers.* Washington, DC: National Air and Space Museum, 1994.
Contains background information and suggestions for activities relating to various spaceflight topics.

———. *Destiny in Space.* Washington, DC: National Air and Space Museum, 1994.
This is a booklet of activities that corresponds with the IMAX video.

Smith, Ron. *Astronaut Foods: The History of Food in Space.* Boulder, CO: American Outdoor Products, 1988.
Available through the Civil Patrol educational resource catalog.

Space Flight: The First Thirty Years. Washington, DC: NASA, 1991.
An excellent source of information containing many photos and graphics.

Sumners, Dr. Carolyn. *Toys in Space: Exploring Science with the Astronauts.* Blue Ridge Summit, PA: TAB Books, 1994.
The physics of how toys operate both on Earth and in space using various scientific principles, including Newton's laws of motion.

Vaden, Judy. *Flight: A Thematic Unit.* Huntington Beach, CA: Teacher Created Materials, 1991.

VanCleave, Janice. *Gravity.* New York: John Wiley, 1993.
The topic of gravity is broken down into smaller units with a series of experiments.

Vogt, Gregory L., and Michael J. Wargo. *Microgravity: Teacher's Guide with Activities for Physical Science.* Washington, DC: NASA, 1995.

Walpole, Brenda. *175 Science Experiments to Amuse and Amaze Your Friends.* New York: Random House, 1988.

Young Astronaut Program. *Flight in the Atmosphere.* Vol. 5. Washington, DC: Young Astronaut Council, April 1990.

Young Astronaut Program. *The Shuttle: Its Purpose and Parts.* Vol. 5. Washington, DC: Young Astronaut Council, January 1990.

Young Astronaut Program. *You Are Go for Launch.* Vol. 5. Washington, DC: Young Astronaut Council, February 1990.

Why Do I Need a Spacesuit, a poster with suggested activities. Write to: Education Outreach Coordinator, Life Sciences Program Integration Office, NASA–Ames Research Center, Mailstop 239-11, Moffett Field, CA 94305.

Electronic Sources

Doody, Dave, and George Stephan. 1997. *Basics of Space Flight Learner's Workbook.* URL: http://www.jpl.nasa.gov/basics (Accessed August 7, 1997).

Dumoulin, Jim. 1997. *Space Shuttle News Reference Manual.* URL : http://www.ksc.nasa.gov/shuttle/technology/sts-newsref/stsref-toc.html (Accessed August 8, 1997).
Click into any area. Contains an enormous amount of information about the space shuttle.

Dunbar, Brian. 1997. *NASA Mission Patches.* URL: http://www.hq.nasa.gov/office/pao/History/mission_patches.html (Accessed August 8, 1997).

Enticknap, Sarah. 1997. *Astronaut Fact Book.* URL: http://www.jsc.nasa.gov/pao/factsheets/astrofb (Accessed August 15, 1997).
Many links to astronaut information.

———. 1997. *NASA Shuttle Web.* URL: http://shuttle.nasa.gov (Accessed August 8, 1997).
Updates on current shuttle missions with links to past and future missions.

———. 1997. *NASA Shuttle-Mir Web.* URL: http://shuttle-mir.nasa.gov (Accessed August 14, 1997).

Hamilton, Calvin J. 1997. *History of Space Exploration.* URL: http://128.165.1.1/solarsy/history.htm (Accessed August 8, 1997).
This site is good for obtaining research information. There are no graphics.

Launius, Roger D. 1997. *NASA Timeline.* URL: http://www.hq.nasa.gov/office/pao/History/timeline.html (Accessed August 8, 1997).

McDonald, Terry. 1997. *International Space Station.* URL: http://station.nasa.gov (Accessed August 7, 1997).
Click into "Gallery" for photos and "Reference" for facts, FAQs, and acronyms.

———. 1997. *International Space Station Science.* URL: http://station.nasa.gov/science (Accessed August 15, 1997).
Information on the types of science experiments that will take place on the space station.

Smith, Woody. 1997. *Office of Space Flight.* URL: http://www.osf.hq.nasa.gov/Welcome.html (Accessed August 8, 1997).
Links to the shuttle, space station, and the space hotlist.

Wright, Jerry. 1997. *NASA Astronaut Biographies.* URL: http://www.jsc.nasa.gov/Bios/astrobio.html (Accessed August13, 1997).

CHAPTER 6

Responding to Literature

Compare/Contrast

Character Traits

1. Once students have read several myths and legends, have them choose any two of their favorite characters from the stories to compare and contrast, and use the reproducible "Character Traits" (see page 159). Encourage use of the dictionary and thesaurus to enhance vocabulary.

2. Students will then create a chart adapted from *A Literature Unit for d'Aulaires' Book of Greek Myths* to compare and contrast the two characters using the following directions.

   a. Have each student choose three different colors of 9-by-12-inch construction paper, and one piece of 12-by-18-inch construction paper that is a different color than the first three.

   b. Each student will then decide on two different shapes (squares, circles, triangles, etc.).

   c. One shape, along with one of the first three colors, will represent both characters.

   d. The second shape will represent the traits of the two characters, with the second of the three colors used for similar traits, and the third color representing different traits.

   e. Students should cut out the shapes being used for the characters, write the names of each character on the shapes, and place them on the 12-by-18-inch construction paper as shown in the illustration on page 150.

   f. Three to four of the similar trait shapes should be made, cut out, and placed in between the names of the two characters.

g. At least six of the different trait shapes should be cut out and placed on either side of the characters for which these traits are representative.

h. When the charts have been completed, consider having students use these traits to write poems such as limericks, couplets, or cinquains.

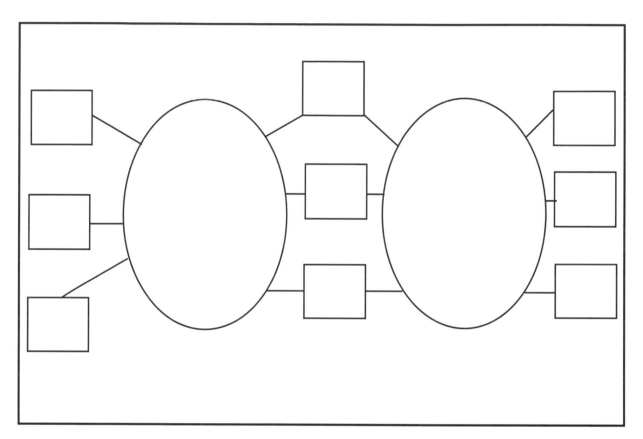

Chart for Comparing/Contrasting Character Traits.

Retelling of Myths and Legends

Have students complete the reproducible "Comparing and Contrasting Versions of the Same Myth or Legend" (see pages 160–61), and work in groups of three or four to create stick-puppet-play reenactments of the different versions of any of the myths and legends.

1. First have students plan and write a short skit for each version of the myth or legend.

2. Using craft sticks or tongue depressors, markers, and a variety of art materials, such as pieces of cloth, wallpaper samples, yarn, etc., students should create the characters for each version of the play. Encourage students to design characters who are the same in both plays a little differently to represent the variations in character traits and/or physical characteristics.

3. Students may design a mural as a backdrop for their play presentations, and present their skits orally, firsthand, or tape each character's part and play the tape while using the stick puppets to act out the scenes.

4. At the end of each group's presentation, have a member of the group ask one of the main characters which version of the story he/she/it prefers to be part of. Another student should have the character respond and tell why he/she/it prefers one version over another.

Reality and Fiction

Of course all the myths and legends are fiction, but there are particular events that occur in these stories that could possibly be real. Students may have a little difficulty discovering some real events, so brainstorm ideas with them first, using any familiar story. The following examples are from *Callisto and Zeus* (see pages 92–93). Real events may be:

➢   hunters would try to shoot a bear

➢   bears are full of fur and have sharp claws

➢   people would be afraid of such a large bear

➢   the big bear and the little bear, as constellations, are near one another

Of course the fictitious events are easier for the students to ascertain.

The following activity helps students identify real and fictional events in stories.

1. Students will be working in groups, and each group will need a large piece of lined or unlined chart paper. Assign each group a different myth or legend.

2. At the top of chart paper, students should write the name of the myth or legend, and divide the paper lengthwise into two columns. One column should be labeled "Real Events" and the other "Fictitious Events."

3. Give each student in the group two sentence strips, so that each student will be able to write one real event on one strip and one fictitious event on the other. Group members should collaborate on thoughts and ideas.

4. Students should then glue the sentence strips onto the chart paper under the proper heading and share the chart with the rest of the class.

Cause and Effect:
Matching Game

As students read the various myths and legends, have them keep a running list of causes and effects from several different legends. Have each group of students, or individual students, create matching games for one different myth or legend with a set of *effect* cards and a set of *cause* cards. Place the card games in a center for students to use at designated times or use as a comprehension review.

Poetry

Reading Poetry

➤ *Choral Reading*

Choose a poem, practice a choral reading with students, and tape students doing the choral reading. Have them listen for ways to improve, practice the improvements, and re-tape. Add motions and/or have small groups illustrate a section of the poem. As the tape is played, show the illustration that corresponds to each verse or section as it is read, or have students perform the motions.

➤ *Dramatization*

This may be a simple or an elaborate activity. As a simple activity, have students work in small groups with one person being the reader. The other group members take parts and perform the action occurring in the poem, or become objects mentioned in the poem. To make it more elaborate, students may create simple props or costumes.

➤ *Painting Poetry*

Read an illustrated poem aloud to the class, but do not share the illustration. Have students create their own interpretation of the poem using watercolors or poster paint, and when students have completed this task, show them the illustration and compare/contrast the artwork.

Poetry Patterns

➤ *Limericks*

Read aloud several limericks to introduce them to students, especially those written by Edward Lear. As you read, ask students to attempt to identify the basic pattern for limericks. They can usually come up with some of the basics, but you will probably need to fill in the details.

Limericks

A limerick has five lines.

Lines 1, 2, and 5 rhyme.

Lines 3 and 4 rhyme and are generally shorter than lines 1, 2, and 5.

Student Limerick Examples

> *There once was a man named Orion.*
> *He was so brave, he killed a lion.*
> *He had a great might,*
> *He knew how to fight.*
> *When Diana shot him, he was dyin'.*
>
>
> Written by Steven Page, Grade 4,
> Tatem Elementary School, March 1996.

> *Andromeda was a helpless maiden*
> *Her life was going to be fadin'*
> *She acted quite brave*
> *Then she was saved.*
> *Andromeda the beautiful maiden.*
>
>
> Written by Mackenzie Lovell, Grade 4,
> Tatem Elementary School, March 1997.

➤ *Haiku*

Haiku is a Japanese form of poetry usually with nature as its topic. Read some Haiku aloud to students and ask them to discover the pattern. Because of its beautiful photographs of nature, two books written by Ann Atwood (see the bibliography at end of chapter) are excellent haiku to share with students.

Haiku Pattern

A Haiku poem has only three lines.

Lines 1 and 3 contain five syllables.

Line 2 contains seven syllables.

The haiku may relate a simple feeling or story.

Student Haiku Example

> *The stars are shining*
> *bright, and night has just begun.*
> *We're ready for the moon.*
>
>
> Written by Sarah Mussoline, Grade 4,
> Tatem Elementary School, March 1996.

Because most haiku poems refer to nature, this type of poetry fits perfectly with any unit in this book. It also gives syllabication practice, as well as vocabulary application. I like to have students write their haiku and then illustrate them with watercolors.

➤ Couplets

Couplets are simple, two-line poems whose words rhyme at the end of each line. For example: When I see the light of the silvery moon; / Time for bed, it's really too soon. Supply rhyming dictionaries for student use when writing couplets, or any other type of rhyming poem, easing the process and helping to expand vocabulary.

➤ Pattern or Shape Poems

A pattern or shape poem is written so that the words of the poem not only describe the topic, but form the shape of the topic of the poem. An example would be a star. Brainstorm descriptive sentences, words, or phrases about a star, and then write those sentences, words, or phrases so that the shape of a star is formed. Almost any topic works well with this type of poem, and allows for much creativity.

➤ Onomatopoeia

Onomatopoeia is a poetic form of writing that employs vocabulary that signifies a sound such as *zoom* or *be-ee-eep*, and gives the reader a visual and auditory image. Using topics from nature or weather works well in developing onomatopoeia vocabulary. Give students a topic and brainstorm sound words that would fit the topic. Examples include: a thunderstorm (*crashing, rumbling, splattering*), or the *rustling* wind and *crackling* leaves. Have students create couplets or quatrain poems using the onomatopoeia word list and organize all the poems into a class booklet.

For more ideas with poetry, see *Writing Poetry with Children* or *Calliope*.

Retellings

Movie Time

Using drama is always an entertaining way to encourage students to retell a story accurately. Acting out a story always works well, but try this idea using either traditional or more modern technology.

After you have read a story aloud or students have read a story, direct them to small groups and let them know that they will be producing a very short silent movie of the tale they have just read or heard. Give students the "Movie Time" reproducible (see page 162), and once they have completed this activity, let students know that either you or another student will be photographing them as they are acting out each scene.

➢ Use a Polaroid camera to photograph each scene. Then give students the photos and request that they paste them on posterboard. Underneath each photo students should write a caption or sentence or two describing the scene.

➢ An alternative to the above is *not* to have the group members write the descriptions under each picture after they have pasted the photos on posterboard. Instead, trade the posterboards among groups, and have other group members write captions or descriptions for each photograph.

➢ Do you have a digital camera in your school? Photograph students' scenes using the digital camera, display the photos on the computer, and have students write the captions and/or descriptions. Print it all out and display.

➢ Supplement the use of the digital camera by printing out the photos; giving the photos, out of sequence, to a different group; and having the group members arrange the photos in the proper order and write descriptions.

➢ If you take photos from year to year with a regular camera, try to save some of them, put them into a center, and allow students use them for sequencing practice.

➢ Videotaping is always another choice, and descriptions and captions can be recorded.

Storylines

Fostering critical thinking and application of retelling skills are enhanced when students complete a storyline activity. To complete this task, students should first make a list, in order, of five to eight major events from the story. Then give students an 18-by-24-inch piece of construction paper or posterboard, and advise them to complete the following procedure.

1. Hold the paper horizontally, place the name of the story at the top of the paper, and draw a straight line across the middle of the paper.

2. Students will decide on the level of emotion created by each of the major situations of the story. The middle line is just that, a neutral feeling created by the event; the farther one goes above the line, the higher and more positive the

emotion, and the farther one goes below the line, the lower and more negative the emotion.

3.   Students will decide what the level of emotion is for each event, and each event will be written and placed somewhere on, above, or below the storyline, in proper sequence. (See illustration below.)

4.   Once completed, lines should be drawn to connect all the events, and illustrations may be added.

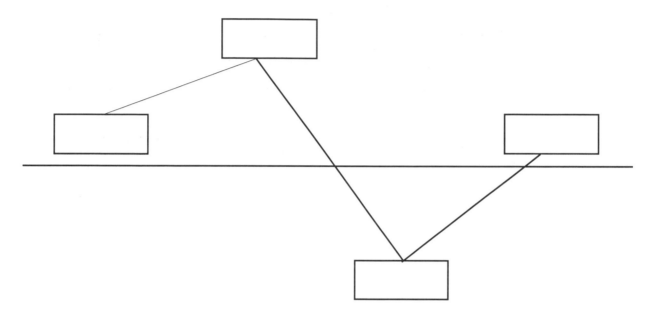

Storyline Example.

Reading and Writing Dialogue

To introduce students to the concepts of reading and writing dialogue, start with a familiar story which contains a good amount of dialogue, and test some of these suggestions.

1.   Take a page or two of a story students are currently reading, or one that has been read recently, place it on a transparency, and give a copy to each student.

2.   Have students circle or mark parts of the dialogue that are unique to dialogue writing, and discuss the items selected and how they are unique to dialogue writing.

3.   Be sure to have students note how a reader can tell who is talking, especially when there is no speaker tag.

4. Based on the information that has been discussed, ask students if they can begin to formulate some simple rules for writing dialogue. Write these on a chart or type them on the computer, to be revised, as new discoveries about writing dialogue are found.

5. Continuing to use the same story, give students a different page of dialogue that has been rewritten so that it does not include the correct capitalization and punctuation, and have them place these items correctly.

6. For a hands-on activity, try this: Give students another page of incorrectly written dialogue, a container of elbow macaroni, glue, and sentence strips. Working in groups or individually, have students rewrite the sentences on the strips, use the macaroni for quotation marks and commas, and place the completed sentence strips on chart paper. Students will need to place other punctuation marks and capital letters correctly with a marker or pencil.

7. Follow up with a revision of the rules for reading and writing dialogue, and assign a writing activity that includes a dialogue writing requirement.

8. Also, at some point, have students search through stories or books they are reading for speaker tag words, such as *exclaimed*, *requested*, *hollered*, etc., and make a list of these words to display in the classroom. Encourage the use of this vocabulary for dialogue writing so that *said* and *asked* are not overused.

Similes and Metaphors

As with dialogue, introduce similes and metaphors through the class's current piece of literature, and start with similes because they are usually easier to identify. Read aloud or display a series of similes, and ask students if they are able to recognize any pattern to the writing of similes. Have students search for similes in their current piece of literature and also list familiar similes. Do the same with metaphors, and have students complete the "Identifying Similes and Metaphors" reproducible (see page 163). Encourage the recognition and use of this type of descriptive writing whenever possible.

Paragraph Writing

Writing a paragraph and sticking to the main idea can be difficult for students, so it is usually necessary to have students break down the paragraph topic and list the details before putting all the ideas together. Try having students use the "Planning for Paragraph Writing" reproducible (see page 164) to plan their paragraphs before writing. After some practice, you will notice that students begin to recognize where to break for new paragraphs when completing longer pieces of writing.

Prediction

To assist your students with forming sensible predictions and drawing conclusions, try the concept of building blocks and the idea that one thing leads to another. The reproducible "Prediction Building" (see page 165) can be used as is, or, for a hands-on activity, use the reproducible as a planning sheet. Then have students cut out large squares of construction paper, write on them, and paste the squares onto another piece of construction paper to display the building blocks of forming a prediction. Each of the bottom four boxes represent events that have taken place. Two of those events lead to another one, as do the next two on the bottom row. The two events in the middle lead one to draw a conclusion that guides one to a prediction. For a more challenging assignment, have students create four rows, using six event boxes on the bottom row, leading to three events, then two, and then the prediction.

There are many techniques for responding to literature, drawing ideas from all the disciplines. These suggestions are meant to assist you in developing your own methods of supporting students in discovering the pleasures and creativity of reading and responding to literature.

Character Traits

Name _____ Date _____

Directions: Choose two characters from myths and legends you have read.
                List as many character traits for each of them as you can.

Name of character and his/her/its myth or legend	Name of character and his/her/its myth or legend
_____ _____ _____	_____ _____ _____
CHARACTER TRAITS	CHARACTER TRAITS
1. _____	1. _____
2. _____	2. _____
3. _____	3. _____
4. _____	4. _____
5. _____	5. _____
6. _____	6. _____
7. _____	7. _____
8. _____	8. _____
9. _____	9. _____
10. _____	10. _____
11. _____	11. _____
12. _____	12. _____

Comparing and Contrasting
Versions of the Same Myth or Legend

Name _____ Date _____

Directions: Choose a myth or legend of which you have read two different versions.
List their similarities and their differences.

First Version:

Name _____

Author _____

Characters:

     a. _____

     b. _____

     c. _____

     d. _____

Main Ideas of the Story:

     a. _____

     b. _____

     c. _____

     d. _____

     e. _____

Second Version:

Name _____

Author _____

Different Characters:

      a. _____

      b. _____

      c. _____

Different Behavior of Characters Who Are the Same:

      a. _____

      b. _____

      c. _____

      d. _____

Different Main Ideas:

      a. _____

      b. _____

      c. _____

      d. _____

Movie Time

Date _____

Names of Group Members: _____

_____

_____

_____

Name of Story: _____

The story you have just read is about to be made into a silent movie with all of you as the actors and actresses. Complete the following information so that you will be ready to perform.

Main Characters: _____

_____

_____

_____

Major Events: List five or more major events as they occurred in the story. Each event will become a scene to be performed in the movie. Be sure that the last event is the conclusion of the story.

_____

_____

_____

_____

_____

_____

_____

Identifying Similes and Metaphors

Name _____ Date _____

Piece of Literature Being Used _____

Similes	Illustration of Similes	Metaphors	Illustration of Metaphors

Planning for Paragraph Writing

Name _____

Date _____

Paragraph topic: _____

Details: _____

_____

_____

_____

_____

Go back and read the details. Do all the details match the paragraph topic? Do any belong with another topic?

_____

My main idea sentence will be:

_____

_____

_____

_____

My concluding sentence will be:

_____

_____

_____

_____

Prediction Building

Name _____ Date _____

Annotated Bibliography

Atwood, Ann. *Haiku: The Moon of Earth*. New York: Charles Scribner's Sons, 1971.
Contains beautiful photographs to go along with the haiku.

———. *My Own Rhythm: An Approach to Haiku*. New York: Charles Scribner's Sons, 1973.
A sequel to *Haiku: The Moon of Earth*.

Booth, David, comp. *'Til All the Stars Have Fallen: A Collection of Poems for Children*. New York: Puffin Books, 1989.
A compilation of short children's poems, most of which refer to nature. There are good examples of shape poems in this book, too.

Carey, Patsy, Cynthia Holzschuher, and Susan Kilpatrick. *Activities for Any Literature Unit*. Huntington Beach, CA: Teacher Created Materials, 1995.
Just as the title states, the activities are adaptable for just about any piece of literature.

Gruber, Barbara, comp. *Whole Language, Literature, and Cooperative Learning*. Torrance, CA: Frank Schaffer Publications, 1990.

Hansen, Karen, ed. *Great Ideas: From Learning Volume Two Language Arts*. Springhouse, PA: Springhouse, 1986.
Good ideas to adapt for a variety of language skills.

Lipson, Greta Barclay, and Jane A. Romatowski. *Calliope*. Carthage, IL: Good Apple, 1981.
Examples of all types of poetry, and ideas for introducing and writing poetry to and with children.

Macon, James M., Diane Bewell, and MaryEllen Vogt. *Responses to Literature: K–8*. Newark, DE: International Reading Association, 1991.
A variety of literature response activities.

Moore, Jo Ellen, and Joy Evans. *Writing Poetry with Children*. Monterey, CA: Evan-Moor, 1988.
Poetry formats and suggestions for use with children.

Ross, Cynthia. *A Literature Unit for d'Aulaires' Book of Greek Myths*. Huntington Beach, CA: Teacher Created Materials, 1993.
A teacher resource.

Smith, Philip, ed. *Favorite Poems of Childhood*. Mineola, NY: Dover Publications, 1992.

Stevenson, Robert Louis. *A Child's Garden of Verses*. Mineola, NY: Dover Publications, 1992.

Suid, Murray, and Wanda Lincoln. *Book Factory*. Palo Alto, CA: Monday Morning Books, 1988.
Tips on how to create books with students.

Sword, Elizabeth Hauge, ed. *A Child's Anthology of Poetry*. Hopewell, VA: Ecco Press, 1995.
An outstanding variety of poetry that includes Dickinson, Hughes, Keats, Longfellow, Whitman, and many others.

References and Resources

Atwood, Ann. *Haiku: The Moon of Earth*. New York: Charles Scribner's Sons, 1971.
Contains beautiful photographs to go along with the haiku.

———. *My Own Rhythm: An Approach to Haiku*. New York: Charles Scribner's Sons, 1973.
A sequel to *Haiku: The Moon of Earth*.

Gruber, Barbara, comp. *Whole Language, Literature, and Cooperative Learning*. Torrance, CA: Frank Schaffer Publications, 1990.

Macon, James M., Diane Bewell, and MaryEllen Vogt. *Responses to Literature: K–8*. Newark, DE: International Reading Association, 1991.
A variety of literature response activities.

Moore, Jo Ellen, and Joy Evans. *Writing Poetry with Children*. Monterey, CA: Evan-Moor, 1988.
Poetry formats and suggestions for use with children.

Ross, Cynthia. *A Literature Unit for d'Aulaires' Book of Greek Myths*. Huntington Beach, CA: Teacher Created Materials, 1993.
A teacher resource.

Smith, Philip, ed. *Favorite Poems of Childhood*. Mineola, NY: Dover Publications, 1992.

Stevenson, Robert Louis. *A Child's Garden of Verses*. Mineola, NY: Dover Publications, 1992.

Appendix

NASA Teacher Resource Centers

NASA-related educational materials, such as videotapes, slide sets, lithographs, and a wide assortment of publications, are available from the centers listed. Smaller, regional centers, by state, have recently been established.

Alaska, Arizona, California, Hawaii, Idaho, Montana, Nevada, Oregon, Utah, Washington, and Wyoming

NASA Ames Research Center
Teacher Resource Center
Mail Stop 253-2
Moffett Field, CA 94035-1000
415-604-3574

California

NASA Teacher Resource Center for
  Dryden Flight Research Center
45108 N. 3rd Street East
Lancaster, CA 93535
805-948-7347

Connecticut, Delaware, District of Columbia, Maine, Maryland, Massachusetts, New Hampshire, New Jersey, New York, Pennsylvania, Rhode Island, and Vermont

NASA Goddard Space Flight Center
Teacher Resource Laboratory
Mail Code 130.3
Greenbelt, MD 20771-0001
301-286-8570
http://pao.gsfc.nasa.gov

Virginia and Maryland's Eastern Shore

NASA Goddard Space Flight Center
Wallops Flight Facility
Education Complex–Visitor Center
Teacher Resource Lab
Bldg. J-17
Wallops Island, VA 23337-5099
804-824-2297/2298

Colorado, Kansas, Nebraska, New Mexico, North Dakota, Oklahoma, South Dakota, Texas

NASA Johnson Space Center
Teacher Resource Center
Mail Code AP 2
2101 NASA Road One
Houston, TX 77058-3696
281-483-8696

Florida, Georgia, Puerto Rico, Virgin Islands

NASA John F. Kennedy Space Center
Educators Resource Laboratory
Mail Code ERL
Kennedy Space Center, FL 32899-0001
407-867-4090

Kentucky, North Carolina, South Carolina, Virginia, West Virginia

NASA Teacher Resource Center for
　Langley Research Center at the
　Virginia Air and Space Center
600 Settler's Landing Road
Hampton, VA 23669-4033
757-727-0900 (x 757)
http://seastar.vasc.mus.va.us

Illinois, Indiana, Michigan, Minnesota, Ohio, Wisconsin

NASA Lewis Research Center
Teacher Resource Center
Mail Stop 8-1
21000 Brookpark Road
Cleveland, OH 44135-3191
216-433-2017

Alabama, Arkansas, Iowa, Louisiana, Missouri, Tennessee

NASA Teacher Resource Center for
　Marshall Space Flight Center
U.S. Space & Rocket Center
P.O. Box 070015
Huntsville, AL 35807-7015
205-544-5812

Mississippi

NASA Stennis Space Center
Teacher Resource Center
Building 1200
Stennis Space Center, MS 39529-6000
601-688-3338

Any inquiries related to solar system and planetary exploration

NASA Jet Propulsion Laboratory
Teacher Resource Center
JPL Educational Outreach
4800 Oak Grove Drive
Mail Code CS-530
Pasadena, CA 91109-8099
818-354-6916

Other NASA Resources

NASA CORE (Central Operation of Resource for Educators)

A wide variety of multimedia NASA materials are available, for a small fee, through CORE.

NASA CORE
Lorain County JVS
15181 Route 58 South
Oberlin, OH 44074
216-774-1051, (x 249/293)
216-774-2144 (fax)
E-mail: nasaco@leeca8.leeca.ohio.gov
NASA CORE Home Page:
　http://spacelink.msfc.nasa.gov/CORE

NASA Education Division

300 E Street SW
Mail Code FEO
Washington, DC 20546
202-358-1110
NASA Education Home Page:
　http://www.hq.nasa.gov/office/codef/
　education
NASA Home Page: http://www.nasa.gov

NASA Office of Mission to Planet Earth

NASA Headquarters
Code Y
Washington, DC 20546-0001
Use this address when requesting Mission
　to Planet Earth (MPTE) materials.

NASA Quest

NASA Quest is the K–12 Internet Initiative that provides programs and educational opportunities online.

Access to Quest:
    http://quest.arc.nasa.gov
E-mail list:
    listmanager@quest.arc.nasa.gov
In body of message, type:
    subscribe sharing-nasa
E-mail: info@quest.arc.nasa.gov

NASA Spacelink

Spacelink is an electronic source of educational information.

World Wide Web:
    http://spacelink.msfc.nasa.gov
Gopher: spacelink.msfc.nasa.gov
Anonymous FTP:
    spacelink.msfc.nasa.gov
Telnet: spacelink.msfc.nasa.gov
TCP/IP address: 192.149.89.61
E-mail: comments@spacelink.msfc.nasa.gov
Regular Mail: NASA Spacelink
    Education Programs Office
    Mail Code CL 01
    NASA Marshall Space Flight Center
    Huntsville, AL 35812-0001
    205-961-1225

Additional Aerospace Resources

Astronomical Society of the Pacific

390 Ashton Avenue
San Francisco, CA 94112
800-335-2524

The Boeing Company

Public Relations Department
P.O. Box 3707
Seattle, WA 98124

Challenger Center for Space Science Education

1029 North Royal Street
Suite 300
Alexandria, VA 22314
703-683-9740
703-683-7546 (fax)
website: http://www.challenger.org

Civil Air Patrol (CAP) National Headquarters

Aerospace Education Division
105 South Hansell Street
Building 174
Maxwell Air Force Base, AL 36112-6332

Civil Air Patrol Aerospace Education Regional Offices

Contact the CAP regional office nearest you for aerospace educational materials or information related to aerospace education.

Great Lakes Region: Illinois, Indiana, Kentucky, Michigan, Ohio, Wisconsin

Ms. Alice Noble
Det 3/CAP-USAF GLLR
5400 Skeel Avenue/Suite 2
Wright-Patterson Air Force Base, OH
    45433-5239
937-257-6836
E-mail: Noble@110smtp.wpafb.af.mil

Middle East Region: Delaware, District of Columbia, Maryland, North Carolina, South Carolina, Virginia, West Virginia

Mr. Robert McManus
1609 Brookley Avenue
Andrews Air Force Base, MD
    20762-5000
301-981-0166
E-mail: mcmanus@juno.com

North Central Region: Iowa, Kansas, Minnesota, Missouri, Nebraska, North Dakota, South Dakota

Mr. Dennis Yeager
Building 852
Minneapolis, MN 55450-2000
612-725-8246
E-mail: dyeager@msp.afres.af.mil

Northeast Region: Connecticut, Maine, Massachusetts, New Hampshire, New Jersey, New York, Pennsylvania, Rhode Island, Vermont

Dr. Ann Walko
2610 East Second Street
McGuire Air Force Base, NJ 08641-5018
609-724-5674
E-mail: annwalko@juno.com

Pacific Region: Alaska, California, Hawaii, Nevada, Oregon, Washington

Ms. Barbara DeCamp
5934 Price Avenue
Building 1019
McClellan Air Force Base, CA
     95652-1257
916-920-2099
E-mail: BDeCamp@aol.com

Rocky Mountain Region: Colorado, Idaho, Montana, Utah, Wyoming

Dr. Ben Millspaugh
7245 East Irvington Place
Denver, CO 80220-6911
303-676-3082
E-mail: Benton.ae@juno.com

Southeast Region: Alabama, Florida, Georgia, Mississippi, Puerto Rico, Tennessee

Mr. Eugene Stepko
105 South Hansell Street
Building 714
Maxwell Air Force Base, AL 36112-6332

334-953-4213
E-mail: gstepko@cap.af.mil

Southwest Region: Arkansas, Arizona, Louisiana, New Mexico, Oklahoma, Texas

Ms. Dorothy Warren
USAF/SWLR-CAP
P.O. Box 530653
Grand Prairie, TX 75053-0653
962-266-6829 (x 16)
E-mail: swlr@onramp.net

Civil Air Patrol Supply Depot

14400 Airport Blvd.
Amarillo, TX 79111-1207
800-858-4370
806-335-2416 (fax)
E-mail: bsharpe@depot.cap.af.mil
Request Aerospace Education catalog,
     which contains materials and kits
     related to all areas of aeronautics
     and space education.

Federal Aviation Administration Headquarters

Director of Aviation Education
800 Independence Avenue, SW
Office of Public Affairs
Washington, DC 20591
202-267-3471

Lockheed-Martin Aerospace

P.O. Box 179
Denver, CO 80212
303-455-0611

National Air and Space Museum

Smithsonian Institution
Education Department MRC 305
Room P-700
Washington, DC 20560
202-786-2109
website: http://www.nasm.si.edu

National Science Teachers
Association

1840 Wilson Blvd.
Arlington, VA 22201-3000
703-243-7100
website: http://www.nsta.org

Ninety-Nines, Inc.

P.O. Box 59965
Oklahoma City, OK 73519
International Organization of Women
Pilots-Provide speakers and educational
    materials. There are local and state
    chapters.

TRW Space & Technology Group

1 Space Park
Redondo Beach, CA 90278
213-535-4264
website: http://www.trw.com

U.S. Space Camp

One Tranquility Base
Huntsville, AL 35807
800-63-SPACE
website: http://www.spacecamp.com

Young Astronaut Council

1308 19th Street
Washington, DC 20036
202-682-1984
202-775-1773 (fax)
E-mail: YAC1@aol.com
website: http://www.yac.org

Publications

Astronomy

21027 Crossroads Circle
P.O. Box 1612
Waukesha, WI 53187
800-446-5489
414-796-0126 (fax)
website: http://www.kalmbach.com/
    astro/astronomy.html

Final Frontier

P.O. Box 16179
North Hollywood, CA 91615-6179
800-447-7387
This magazine contains articles regarding
    recent shuttle missions, monthly
    skywatches, and other relevant
    space topics.

Imax Corporation

45 Charles Street East
Toronto, Canada M4Y 1S2
416-960-8509
416-960-8596 (fax)

Odyssey

7 School Street
Peterborough, NH 03458-1454
website: http://www.connriver.net/
    Cobblestone/Odyssey

Ranger Rick

National Wildlife Federation
8925 Leesburg Pike
Vienna, VA 22184
1-800-588-1650
website: http://www.nwf.org/nwf/rrick

Sky & Telescope

Sky Publishing Corp.
49 Bay Street Road
Cambridge, MA 02138
website: http://www.skypub.com

Equipment Resources

Edmund Scientific

101 East Gloucester Pike
Barrington, NJ 08007-1380
609-547-8800
609-573-6295 (fax)
Diffraction grating squares available.
  Request catalog.

Rainbow Symphony

6860 Canby Avenue #120
Reseda, CA 91335
800-821-5122
818-708-8470 (fax)
Prism glasses, eclipse shades, and diffraction
  grating available.

The Weather Channel

Education Department 300
P.O. Box 510243
Livonia, MI 48151
800-294-8219 (x 300)
website: http://www.weather.com
Ask for a catalog of their educational
  materials and a schedule for "The
  Weather Classroom," a short, daily
  television program that provides
  information on a variety of Earth-
  and weather-related topics.

Index

About the Author

Photograph by Kathleen Frank
of Creative Photographs.

Joanne C. Letwinch has taught elementary school for more than twenty years. During her career, she instituted classroom programs in integrated thematic instruction, cooperative learning, multiple intelligences, and authentic assessment. She also has developed interdisciplinary thematic units based on literature, science, social studies, and language skills. Presently, she teaches in New Jersey's Haddonfield Public Schools, where she initiated the Young Astronaut Program.

As a member of the Young Astronauts of New Jersey Executive Council, she received the NJEA Distinguished Service to Education Award in 1991. Joanne has been a presenter at the National Science Teachers Association National Convention and the New Jersey Science Teachers Association Convention.